GLOVEBOX ATLAS

IRELAND

7th edition March 2020

© AA Media Limited 2020
Original edition printed 2004

Cartography:
All cartography in this atlas edited, designed and produced by
the Mapping Services Department of AA Media Limited (A05740).

This atlas contains data available from
openstreetmap.org © under the Open Database License found at
opendatacommons.org

Publisher's notes:
Published by AA Media Limited, whose registered office is
Grove House, Lutyens Close, Basingstoke, Hampshire
RG24 8AG, UK.
Registered number 06112600.

ISBN: 978 0 7495 8229 6

A CIP catalogue record for this book is available from
The British Library.

Disclaimer:
The contents of this atlas are believed to be correct at the time
of the latest revision. However, the publishers cannot be held
responsible or liable for any loss or damage occasioned to any
person acting or refraining from action as a result of any use or
reliance on any material in this atlas, nor for any errors, omissions
or changes in such material. This does not affect your statutory
rights. The publishers would welcome information to correct any
errors or omissions and to keep this atlas up to date. Please
write to the Cartographic Editor, AA Media Limited, Grove House,
Lutyens Close, Basingstoke, Hampshire RG24 8AG, UK.
E-mail: *roadatlasfeedback@aamediagroup.co.uk*

Acknowledgements:
AA Media Limited would like to thank the following for information
used in the creation of this atlas:
Fáilte Ireland (Wild Atlantic Way);
Republic of Ireland census 2016 © Central Statistics Office and
Northern Ireland census 2016 © NISRA (population data);
Irish Public Sector Data (CC BY 4.0) (Gaeltacht);
logainm.ie (placenames);
Outdoor Recreation NI and Sport Ireland (waymarked trails);
The Wildlife Trust; Global Mapping, Brackley;
Roads Service and Transport Infrastructure Ireland.

Printer:
Oriental Press, Dubai.

Contents

Map pages	inside front cover
Route planner	**II**
Key to map symbols	**1**
Road maps 1: 300,000 scale	**2–68**
Index to place names	**69–79**
County and administrative areas	69
Place name index	70–79

T0150415

Scale 1:300,000
4.7 miles to 1 inch
3km to 1cm

Route planner

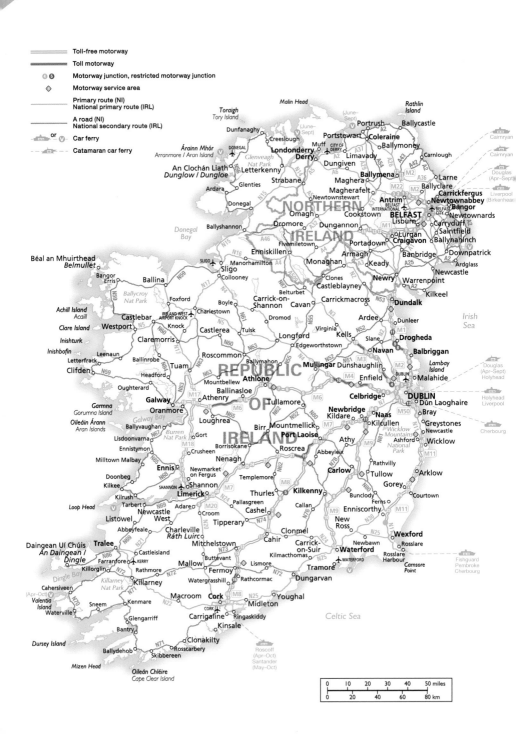

Toll-free motorway
Toll motorway
Motorway junction, restricted motorway junction
Motorway service area
Primary route (NI)
National primary route (IRL)
A road (NI)
National secondary route (IRL)
Car ferry
Catamaran car ferry

Key to map symbols

Motoring Information

M1 — Toll-free motorway	Toll — Bridge or road toll
M1 — Toll motorway	Road tunnel
(1) (2) (1) (2) — Full (1), restricted junction (2)	CORK — Primary destination (selected)
Lusk — Motorway service area	Railway, station, level crossing, tunnel
N17 — National primary route (IRL)	P•R — Park and Ride
N56 — National secondary route (IRL)	C — Crematorium
R182 — Regional road (IRL)	H H — Hospital, with Accident & Emergency
8 — Distance in kilometres (IRL)	International boundary
A4 — Primary route (NI)	Other boundary
A21 — A road (NI)	Airport (major/minor)
B75 — B road (NI)	or — Car ferry
5 — Distance in miles (NI)	Catamaran car ferry
Dual carriageway	or — Passenger ferry
Single carriageway	City, town, village or locality
Roundabout	Beach, other foreshore
Road under construction	628 — Height in metres
Minor road	

Touring Information

Tourist information, seasonal	Shopping centre, sports venue or stadium
Visitor or heritage centre	Golf course
Camping site (AA inspected, Northern Ireland only)	Horse racing, motor-racing circuit
Abbey, cathedral or priory	Boating, skiing activities
Ruined abbey, cathedral or priory	National Trust site (NI/IRL)
Castle, hill-fort	Museum or gallery, Historic house or building
Garden, arboretum	Monument, prehistoric monument
Country park, forest park	Industrial interest, aqueduct or viaduct
Zoo, wildlife or bird park, aquarium	Battle site with date
Theme park, farm or animal centre	Cave, waterfall
Nature, bird reserve	Windmill, distillery or brewery
Wildlife Trust Reserve	Tourist railway, other place of interest
Wild Atlantic Way	World Heritage Site (UNESCO)
Waymarked walk	Boxed symbols indicate attractions within urban areas
Viewpoint, picnic site	Gaeltacht (Irish language area)
Lighthouse, beach	Woodland

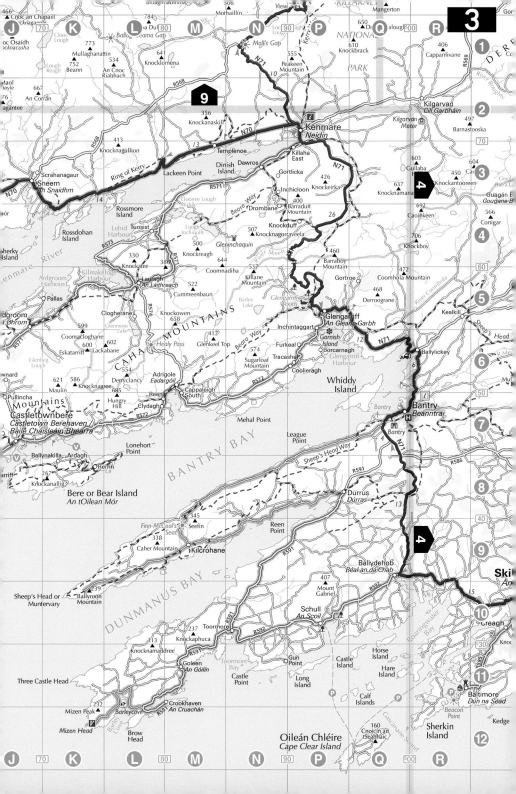

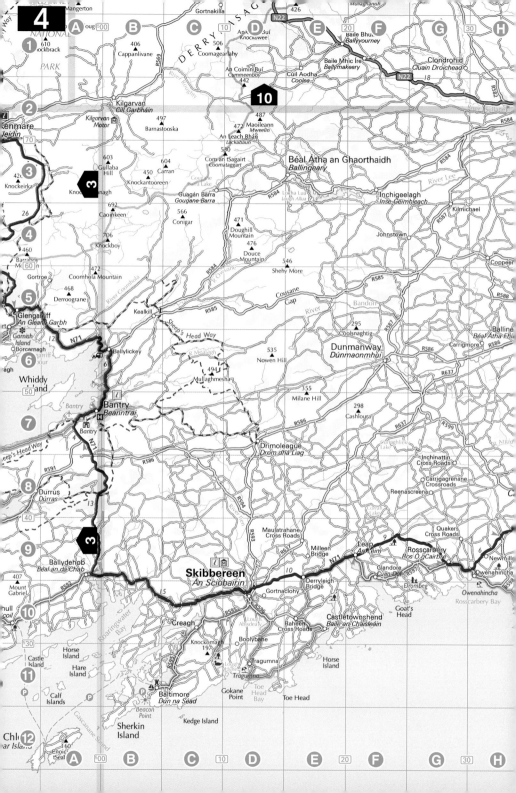

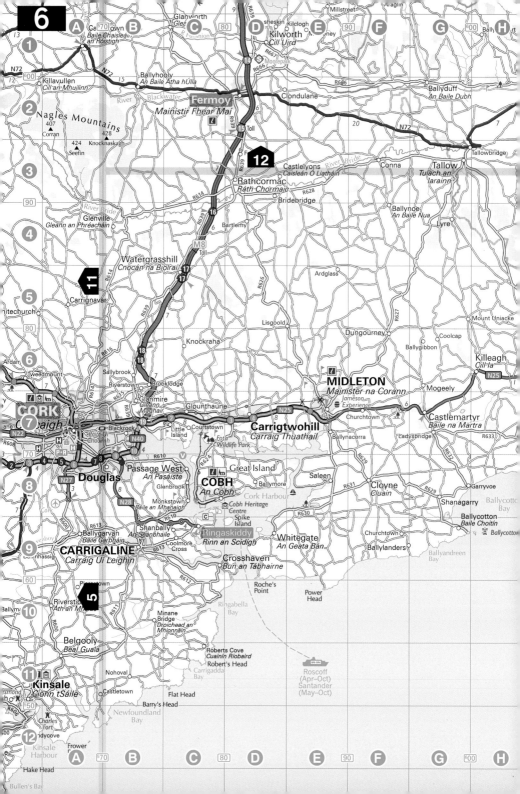

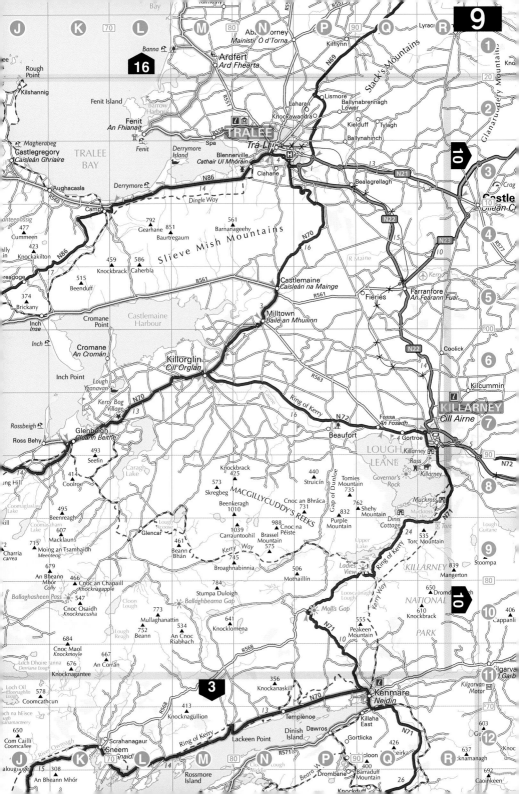

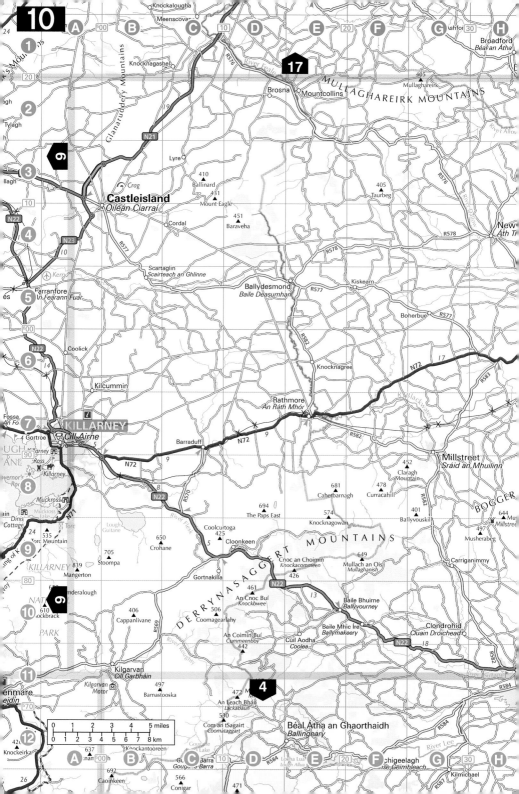

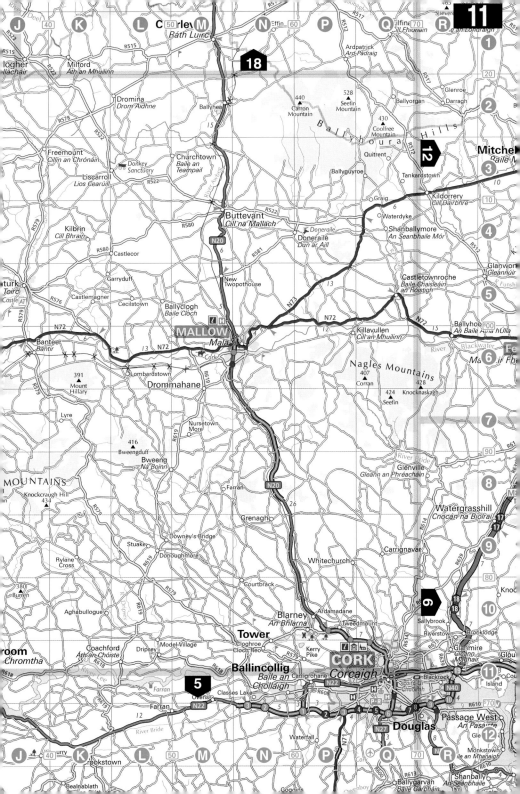

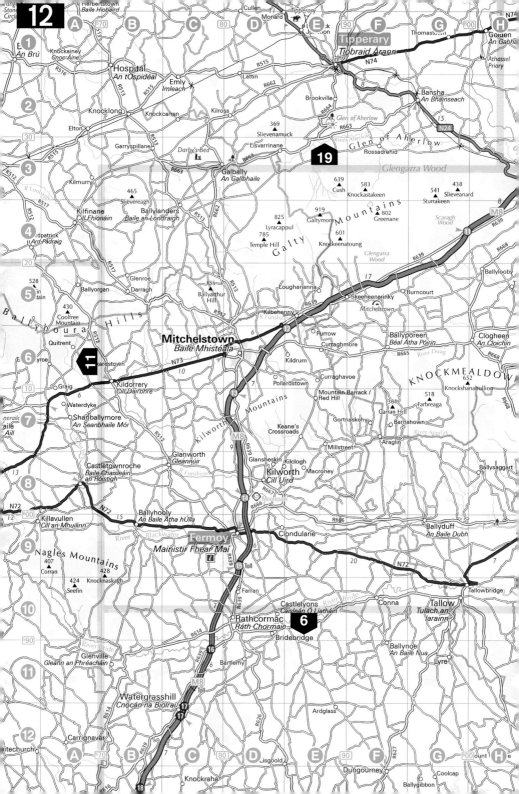

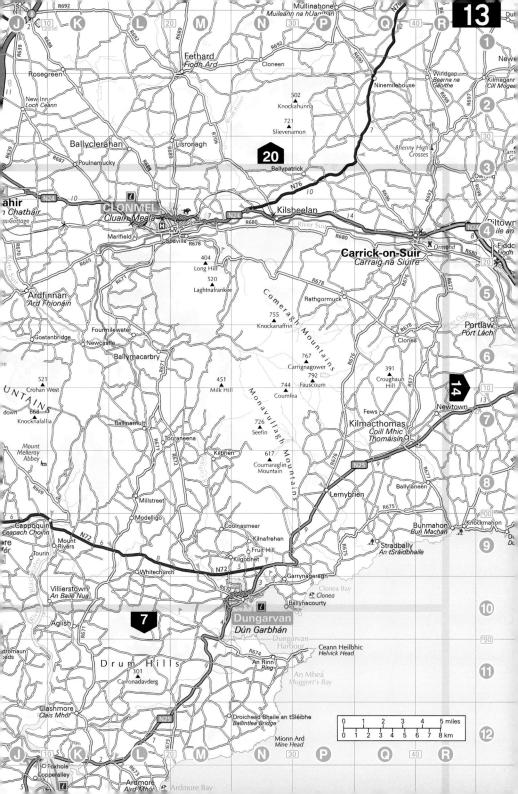

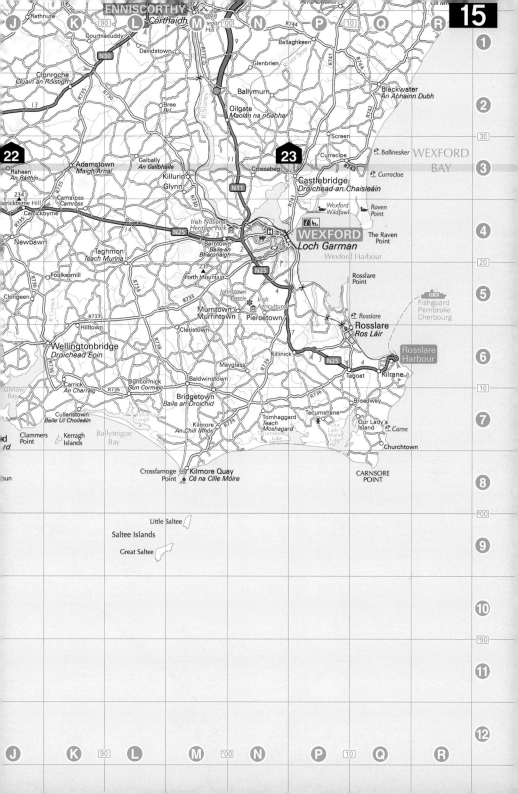

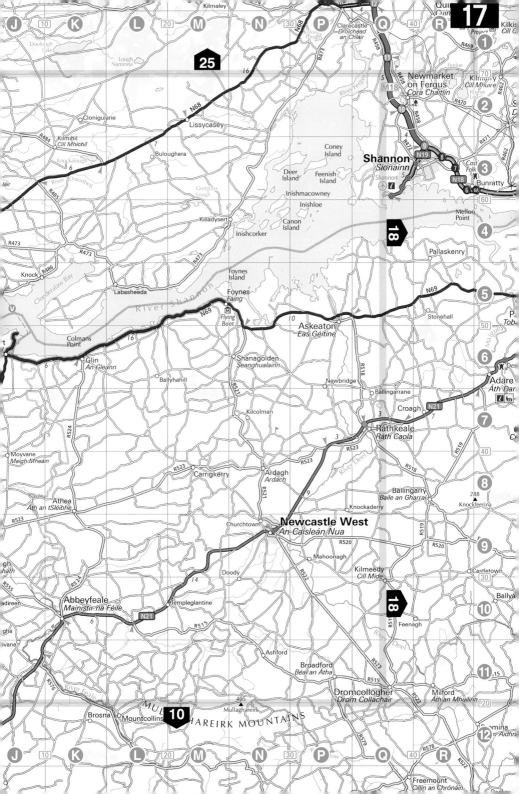

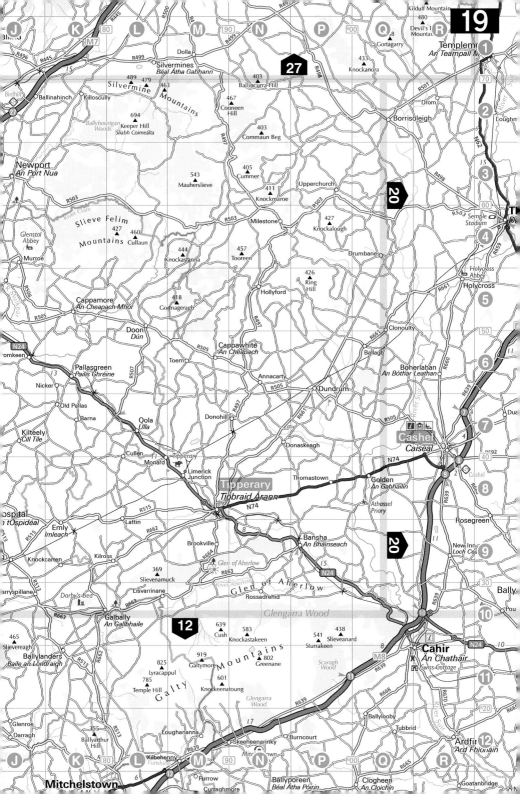

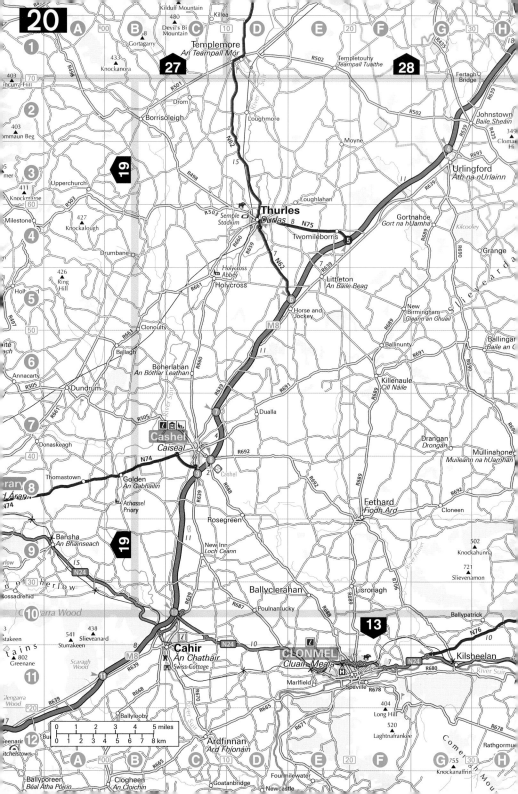

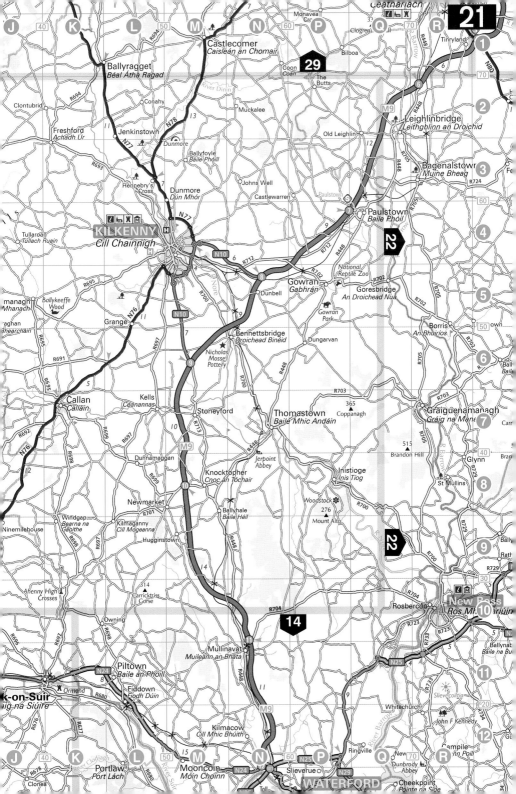

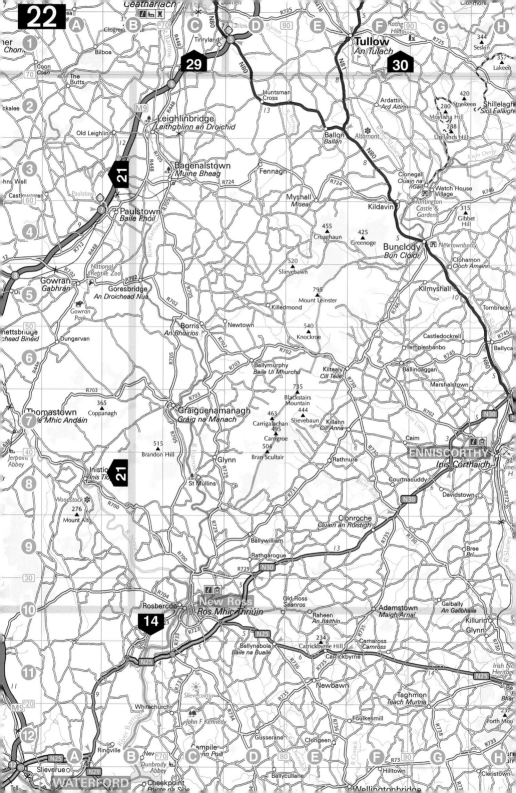

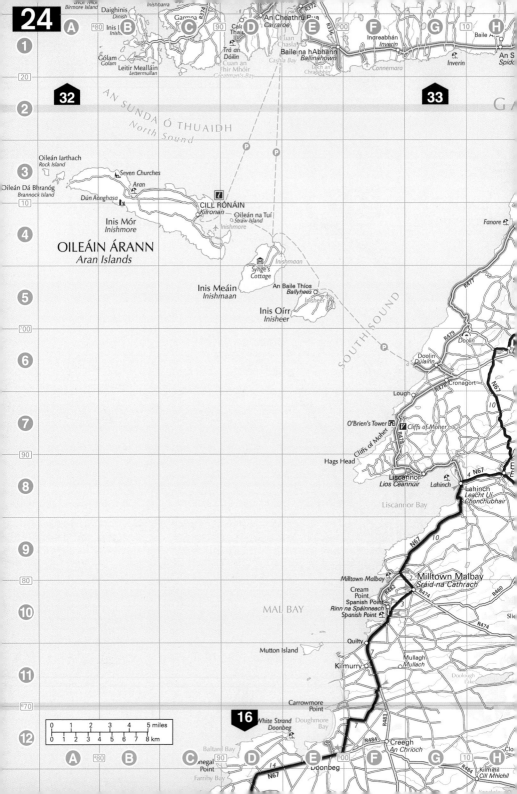

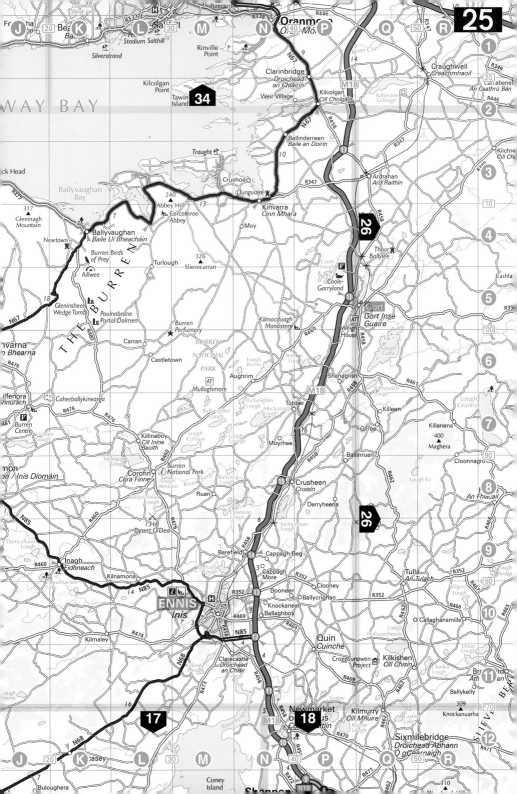

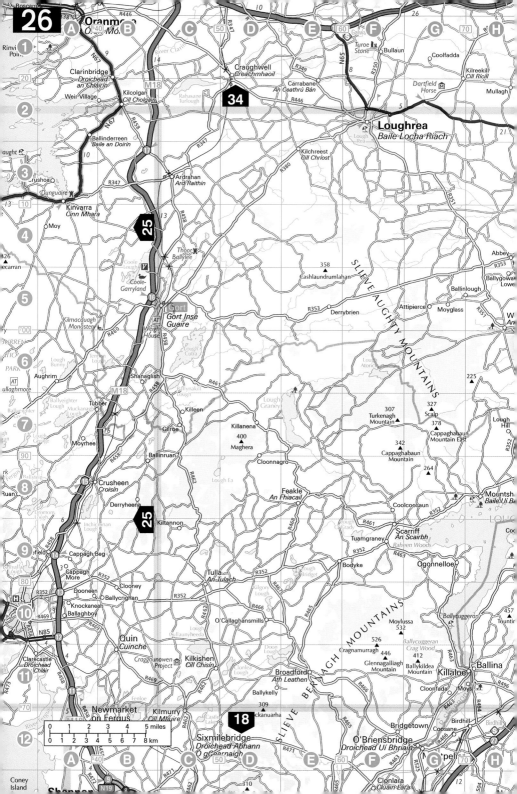

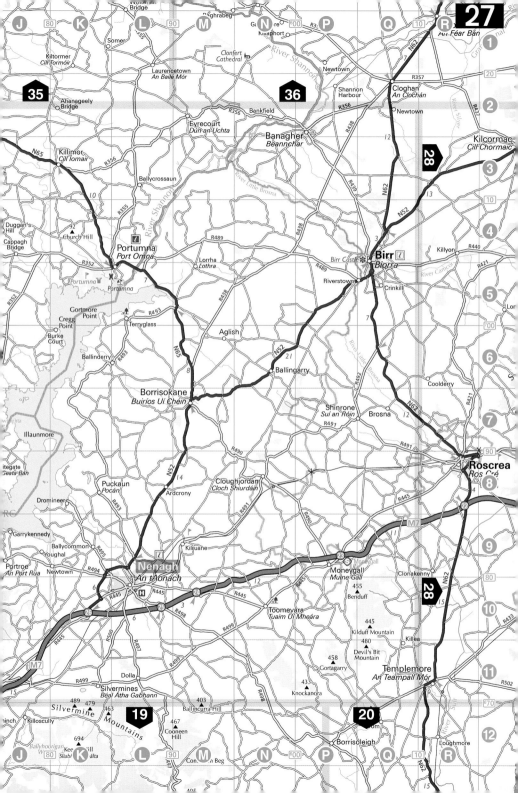

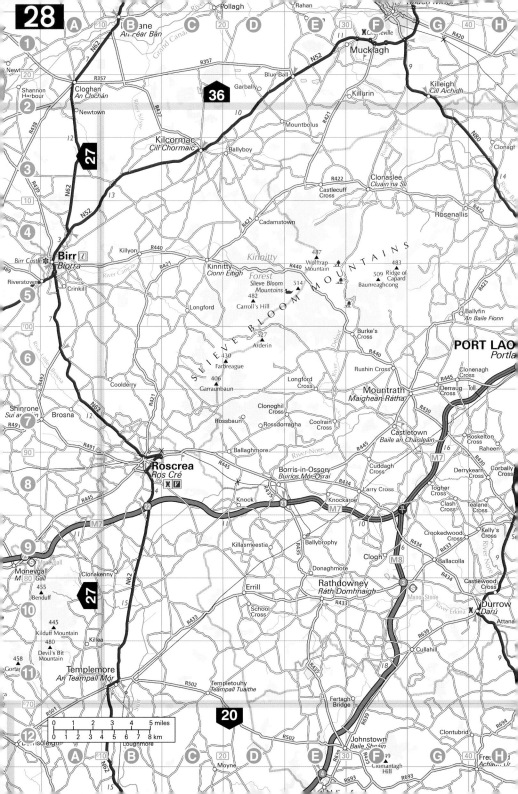

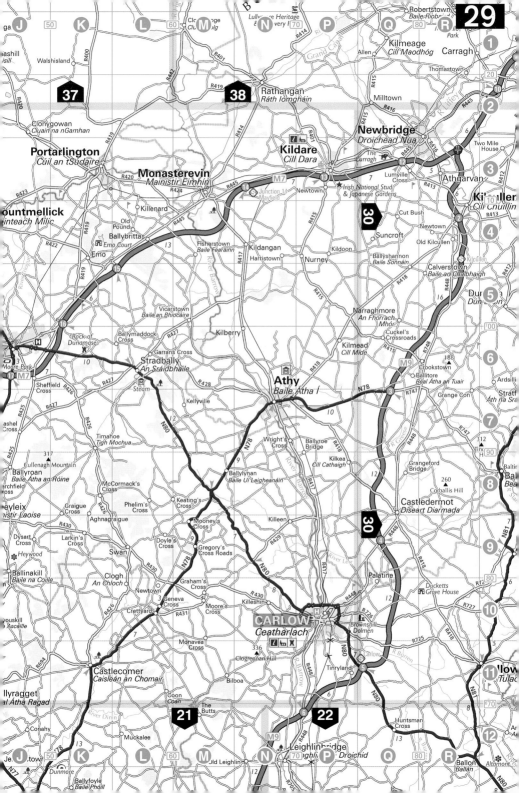

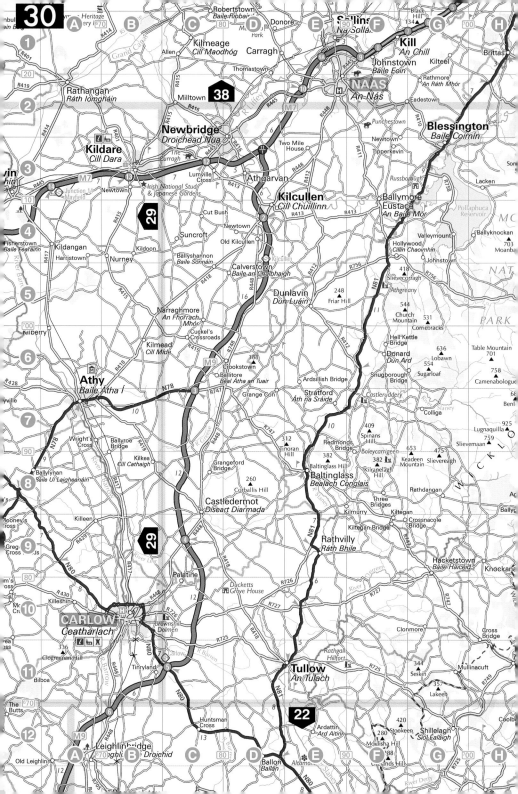

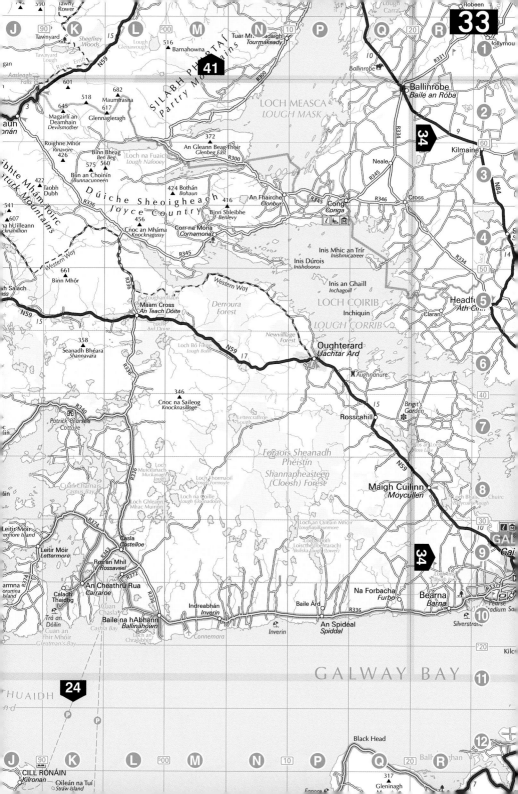

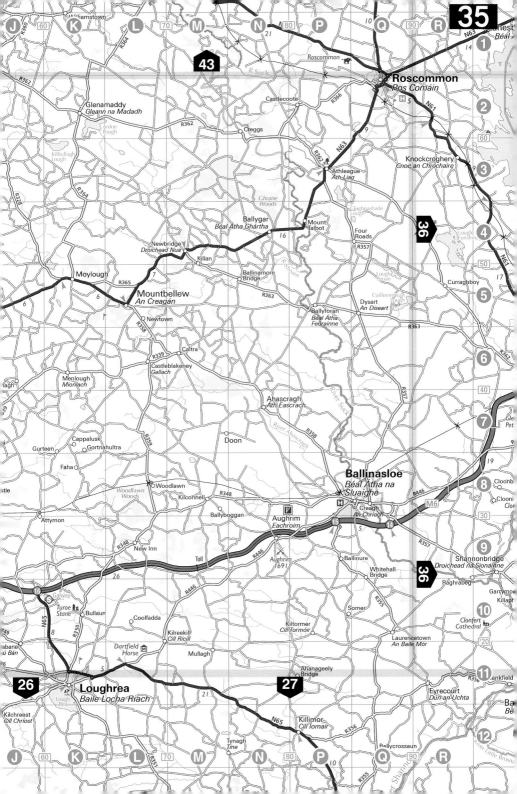

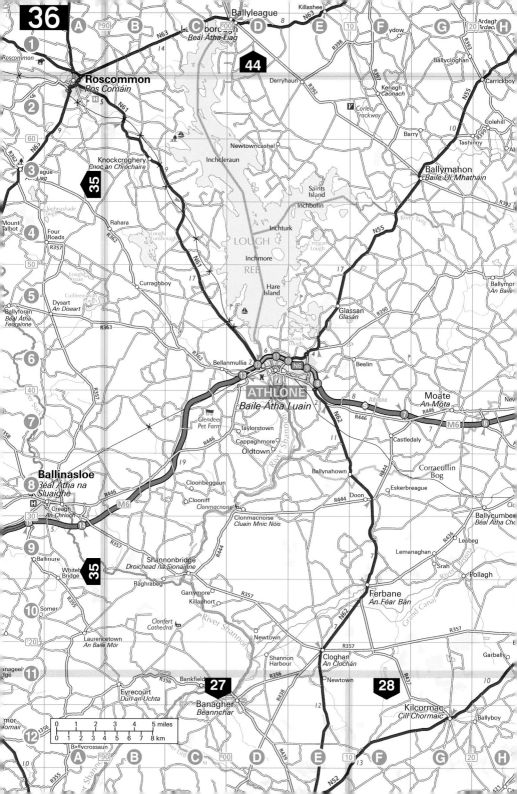

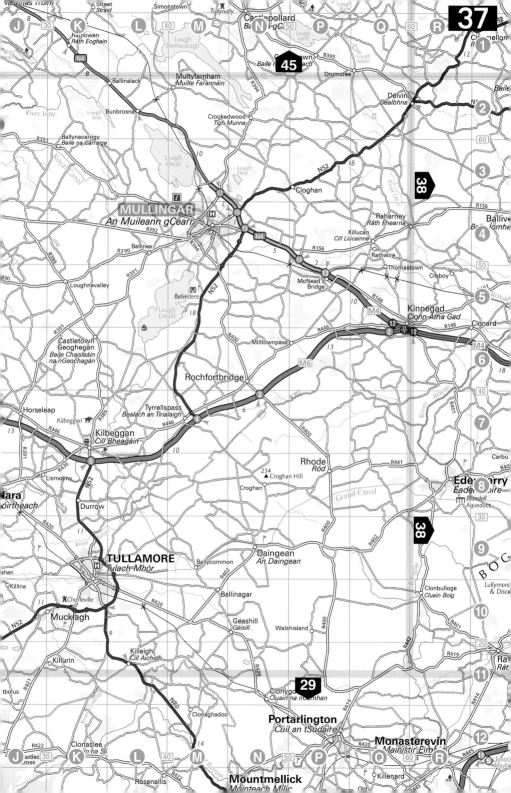

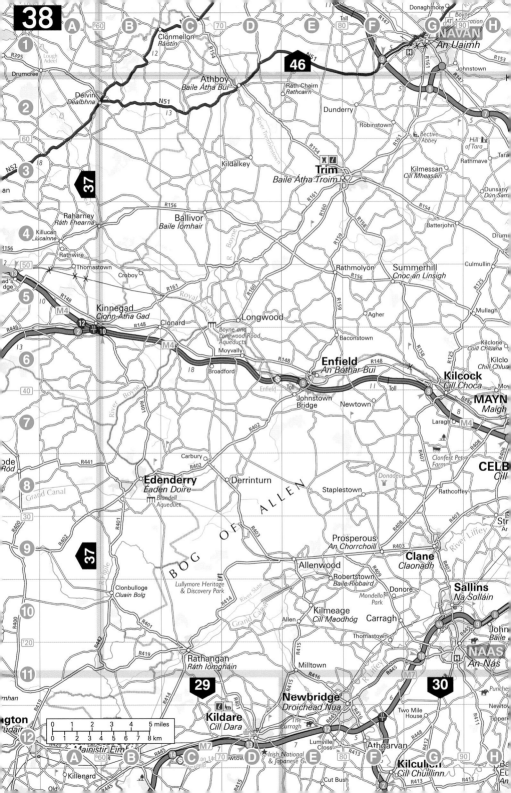

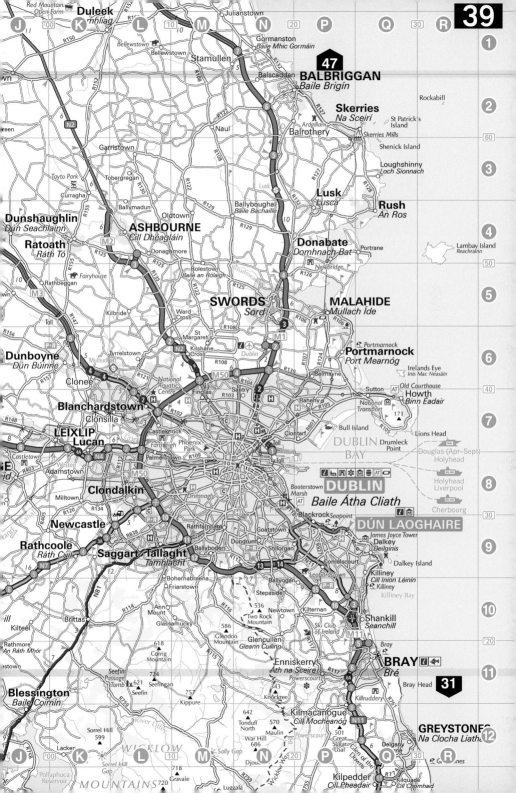

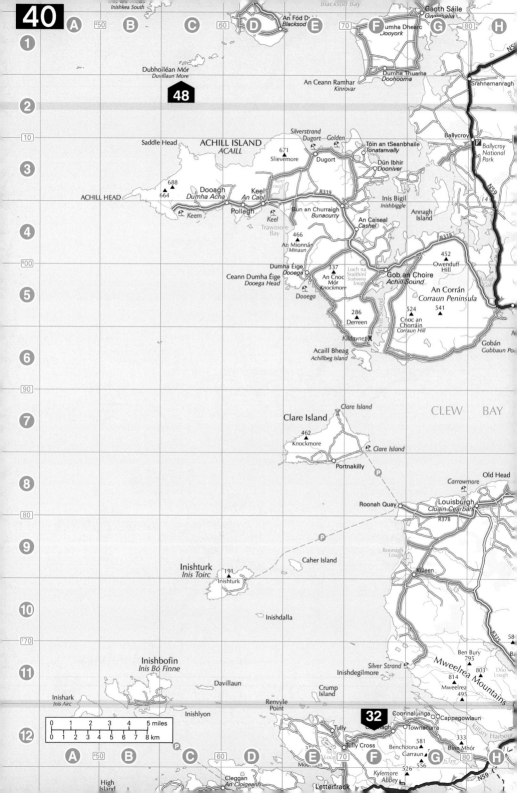

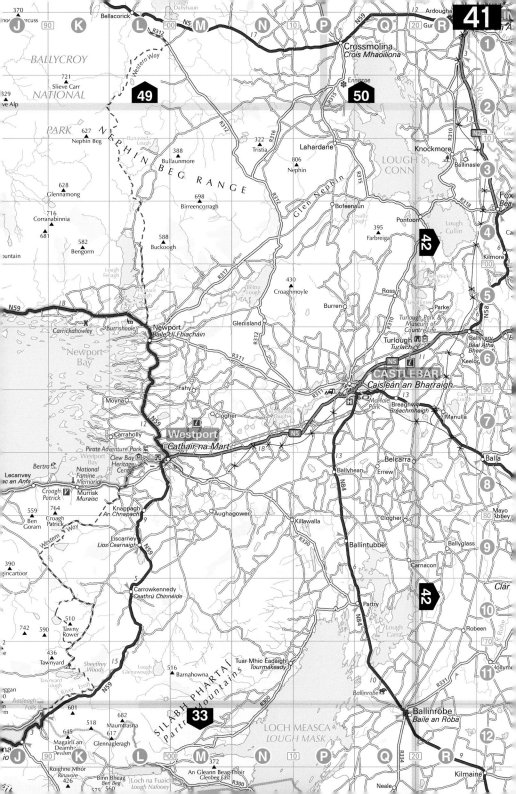

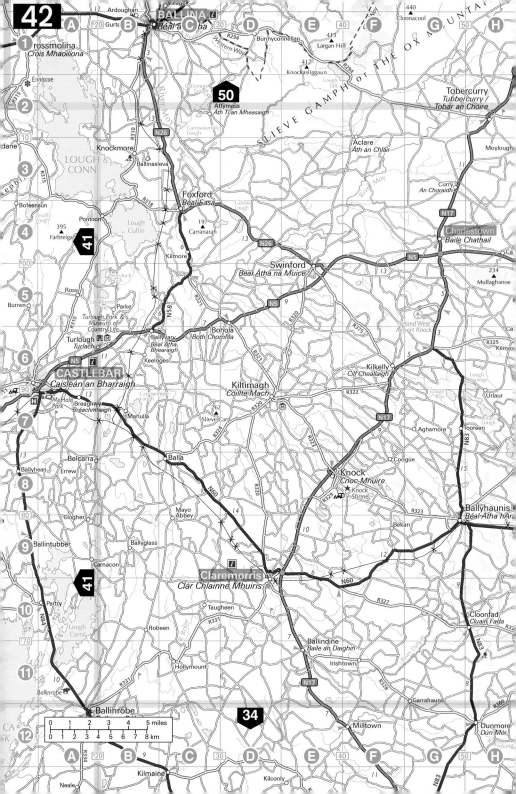

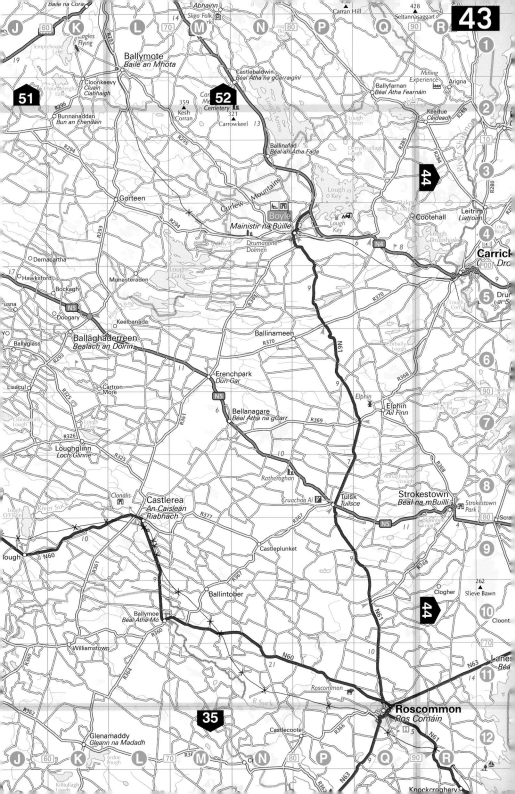

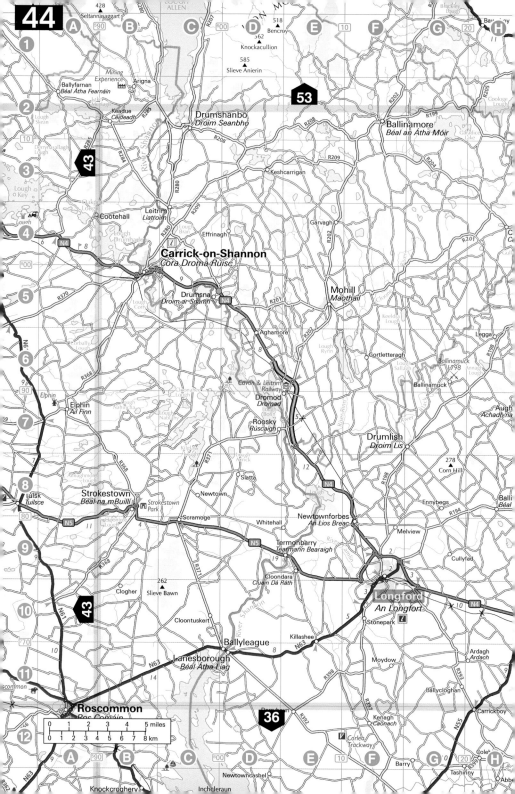

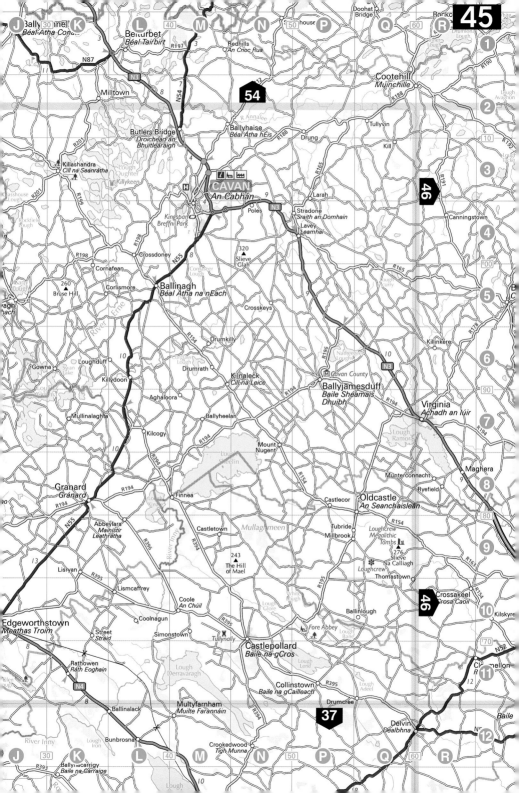

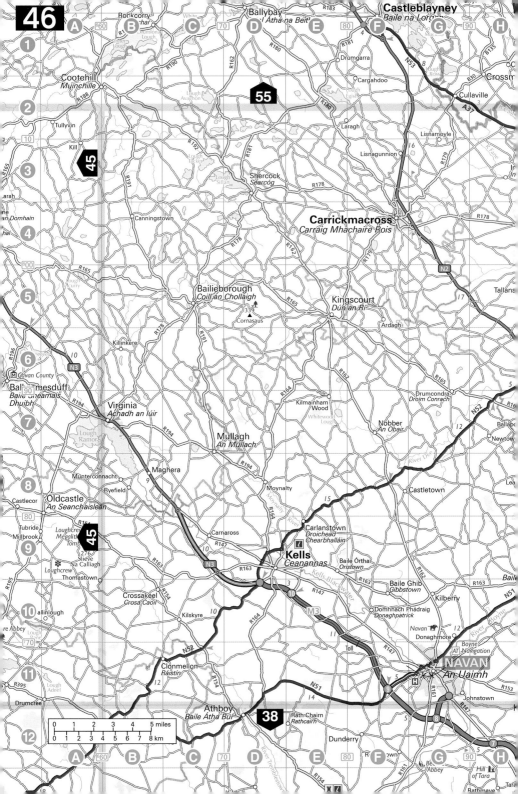

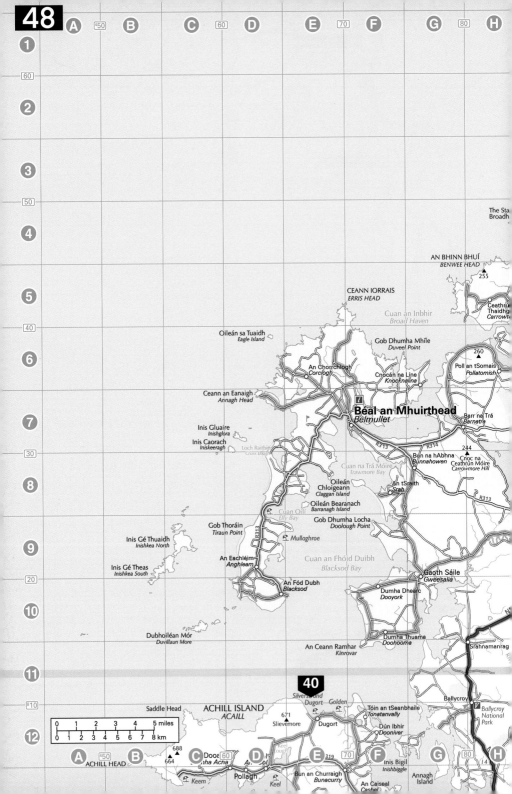

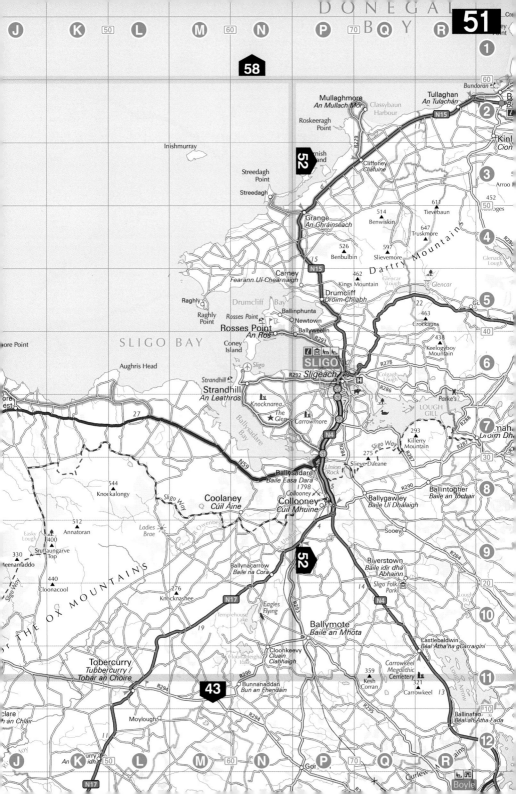

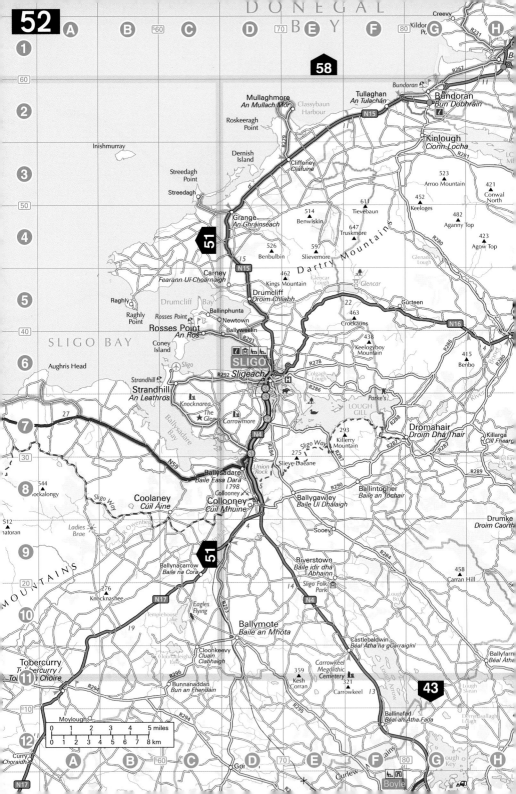

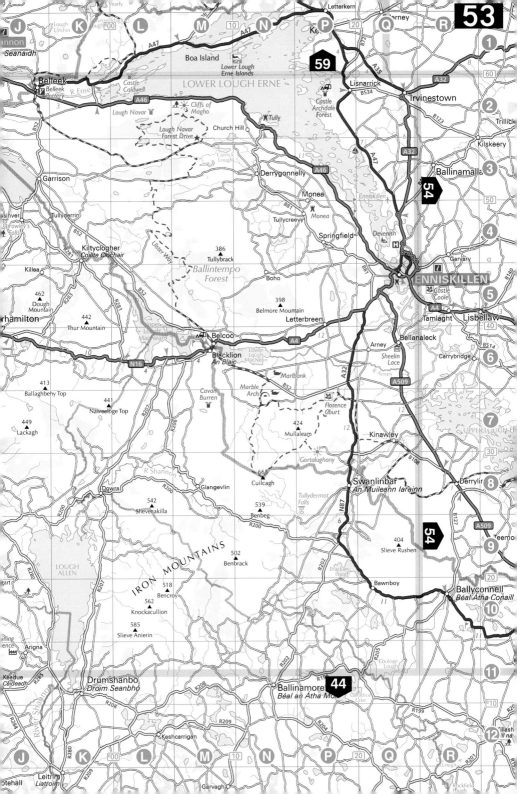

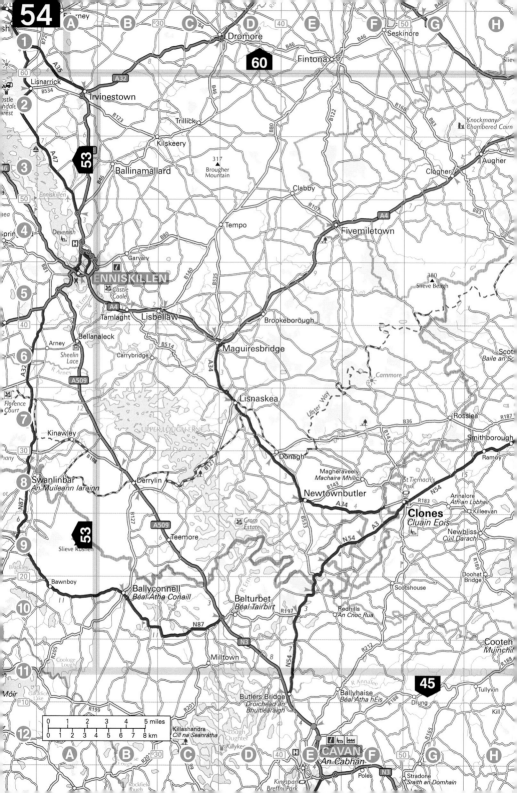

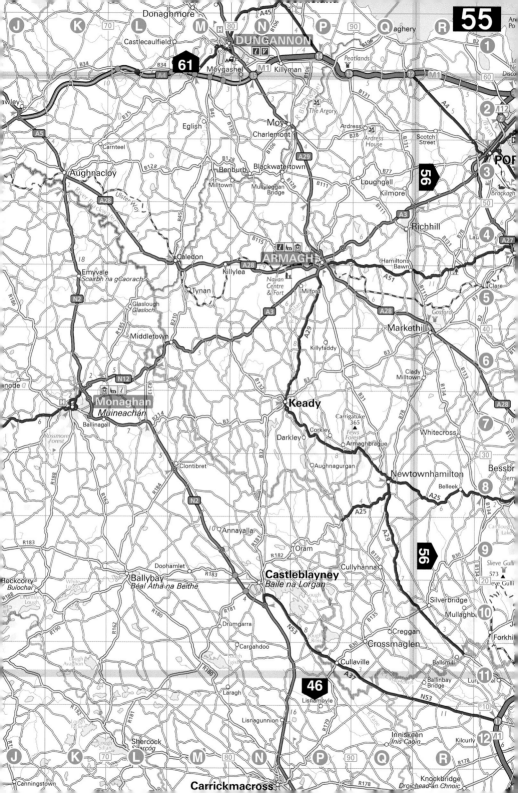

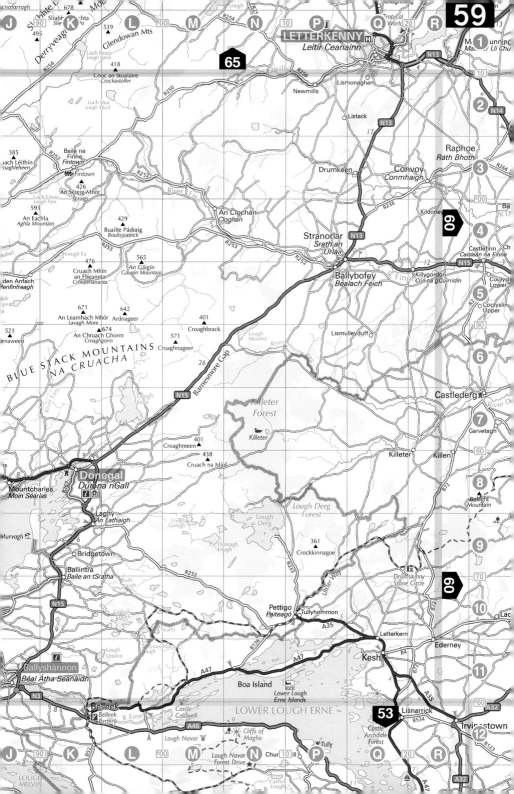

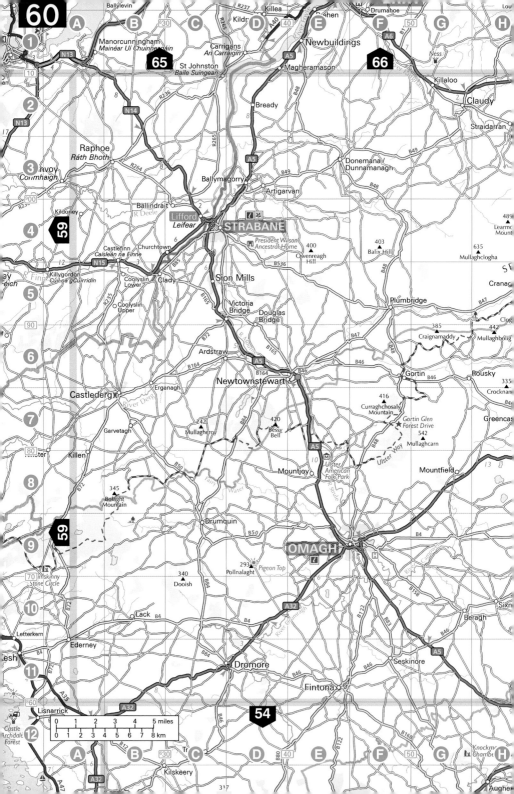

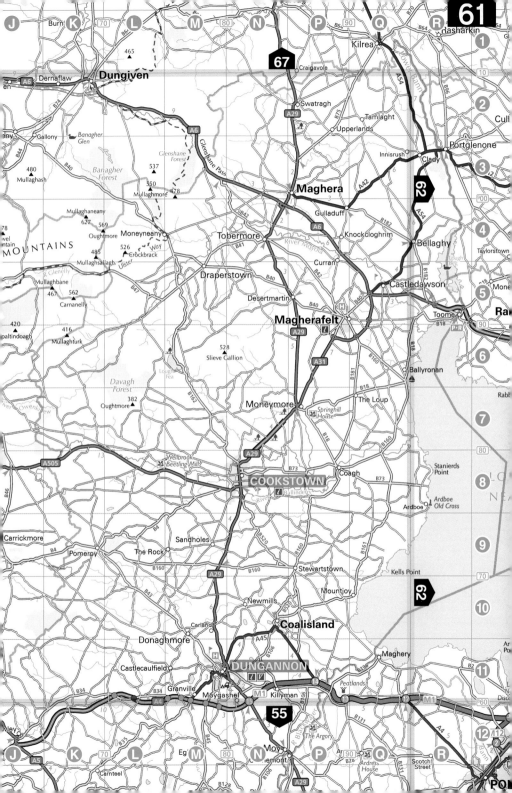

Toraigh
Tory Island

Cainéal Thoraí
Tory Sound

Inis Beag
Inishbeg

Oileán Dúiche
Inishdooey

Inis Bó Finne
Inishbofin

McSwyne's
Gun
Dún

CNOC FOLA
BLOODY FORELAND

Bá Bhaile
an Easa
Ballyness
Bay

Ráith
Ray

314
Cnoc Fola
Bloody
Foreland

Machaire
Rabhartaigh
Magheraroarty

Cill Ulta
Killult

An Fál Carrach
Falcarragh

Bun na Leaca
Brinlack

Inis Oirthir
Inishsirrer

Gort an Choirce
Gortahork

Gaoth Dobhair
Gweedore

Inis Meáin
Inishmeane

R256

Gabhla
Gola Island

Loch Lacha
Lough Lagha

Doirí Beaga
Derrybeg

429

Taobh an Leithid
Tievealehid

564

Inis Fraoigh
Inishfree Lower

R257

An Bun Beag
Bunbeg

425

584 603

Uaigh
Owey Island

R258

Gaoth Dobhair
Gweedore

3

Loch Alltáin
Altan Lough

Carrickfinn

R257

2

751 555

An Chruit
Cruit Island

Dún na
Donegal

Loch na Cuinge
Lough Nacung

An Earagal
Errigal

An D
Do

Cionn Caslach
Kincasslagh

2

Cróithlí
Crolly

457

The Poisoned Glen
Loch Dhún Lúiche
Dunlewey Lough

486

Anagaire
Annagary

R259

Loch an Iúir
Lough Anure

517 489

Sliabh Dhoire Bheatha
Slieve Dhoire Bheatha

596

Na Rosa
The Rosses

Crocnafarragh

AT

678

Ailt an Chorráin
Burtonport

N56

Lochan Iúir
Loughanure

Sliabh Sneachta
Slieve Snaght

539

Árainn Mhór
Arranmore /
Aran Island

227

12

495

Derryveagh

Glendowan

Mountains

Inis Mhic
an Doirn
Rutland
Island

7

An Clochán Liath
Dunglow / Dungloe

Loch Beara
Lough Barra

418

Inis Caorach
Inishkeeragh

R259

315
Cró Bheithe
Crovely

Cnoc an Stualaire
Crockastoller

R254

Inis Fraoigh
Inishfree Upper

N56

Mhachaire
Mór

58

4

An Dúchoraidh
Doocharry

Loch Muc
Lough Muck

0 1 2 3 4 5 miles
0 1 2 3 4 5 6 7 8 km

Droim Lo
Drumle

An C
Cloghbolie

385

Béal an Bheara

Mín an Chairn
Meenacarn

Bá Uachtair

Baile na
Finne

R252

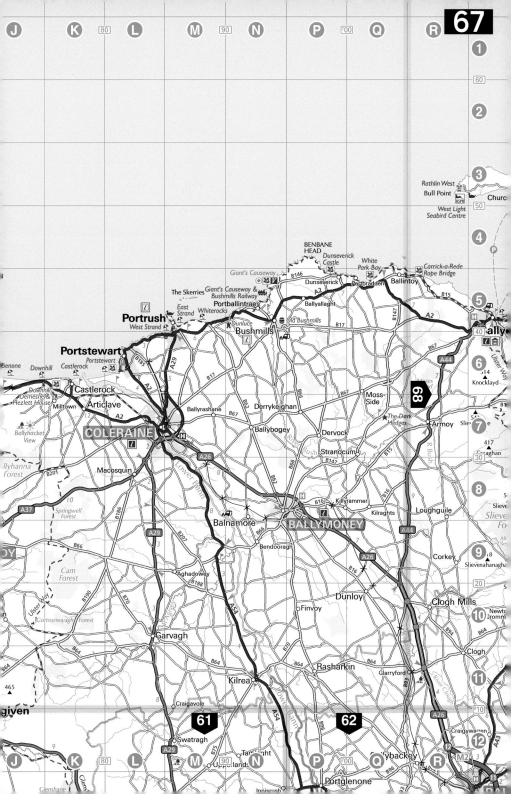

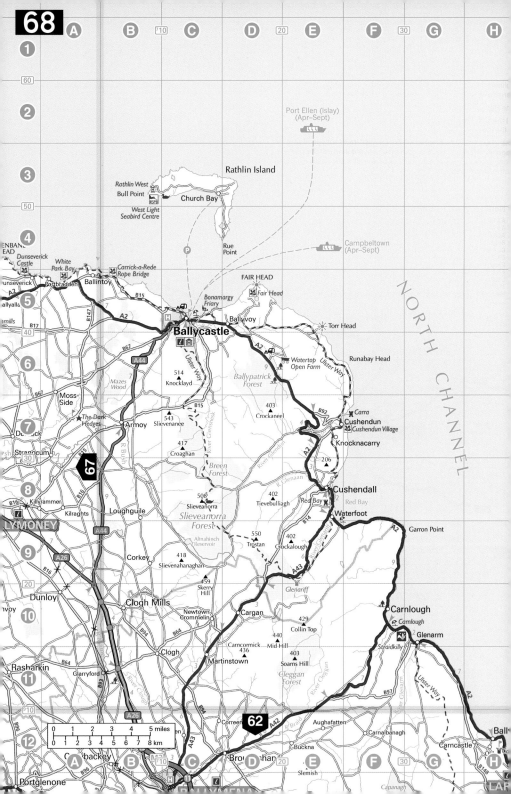

ollowing recent reform there are 11 local government districts in Northern Ireland. The former six counties of Antrim, Armagh, Down, ermanagh, Londonderry and Tyrone are still referred to locally but their use is in decline and they have not been used in this atlas.

he Republic of Ireland is divided into 31 administrative districts which includes 26 counties.

ll the districts for each country are shown on the following map and listed below, together with the abbreviated name which has been used the index.

he index lists places appearing in the main-map section of the atlas in alphabetical order. The reference following each name gives the atlas age number and grid reference of the square in which the place appears.

ore than 75 top places of interest are indexed in **red** or **green** (if a World Heritage site), motorway service areas in **blue**, airports in *blue italic* and ational Parks in *green italic*.

Northern Ireland Districts

A & ND	Ards and North Down
A & N	Antrim & Newtownabbey
AB & C	Armagh City, Banbridge & Craigavon
Belfst	Belfast (1)
CC & G	Causeway Coast & Glens
D & S	Derry City & Strabane
E Antr	Mid & East Antrim
F & O	Fermanagh & Omagh
L & C	Lisburn & Castlereagh City
M Ulst	Mid Ulster
NM & D	Newry, Mourne and Down

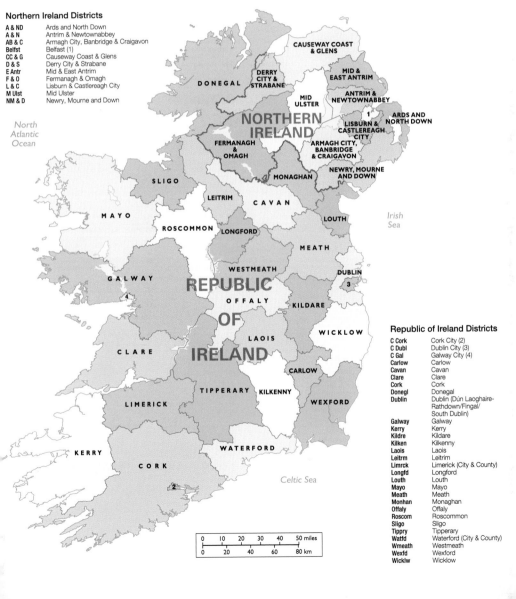

Republic of Ireland Districts

C Cork	Cork City (2)
C Dubl	Dublin City (3)
C Gal	Galway City (4)
Carlow	Carlow
Cavan	Cavan
Clare	Clare
Cork	Cork
Donegl	Donegal
Dublin	Dublin (Dún Laoghaire-Rathdown/Fingal/South Dublin)
Galway	Galway
Kerry	Kerry
Kildre	Kildare
Kilken	Kilkenny
Laois	Laois
Leitrm	Leitrim
Limrck	Limerick (City & County)
Longfd	Longford
Louth	Louth
Mayo	Mayo
Meath	Meath
Monhan	Monaghan
Offaly	Offaly
Roscom	Roscommon
Sligo	Sligo
Tippry	Tipperary
Watfd	Waterford (City & County)
Wmeath	Westmeath
Wexfd	Wexford
Wicklw	Wicklow

A

Abbey Galway....26 H4
Abbeydorney/Mainistir Ó
d'Torna Kerry....16 E11
Abbeyfeale/Mainistir na Féile
Limrck....17 K10
Abbeyknockmoy Galway....34 H6
Abbeylara/Mainistir
Leathrátha Longfd....45 L9
Abbeyleix/Mainistir Laoise
Laois....28 H8
Abbeyshrule Longfd....36 H3
Abington Limrck....19 J5
Acaill/Achill Island Mayo....40 D3
Achill Island/Acaill Mayo....40 D3
Achill Sound/Gob an Choire
Mayo....40 F5
Aclare/Áth an Chláir Sligo....42 F2
Acton AB & C....56 D5
Adamstown Dublin....39 K8
Adamstown/Maigh Arnaí
Wexfd....22 F10
Adare/Áth Dara Limrck....18 D6
Adrigole/Eadargóil Cork.... 3 M6
Aghabullogue Cork....11 K10
Aghadowey CC & G....67 M9
Aghagallon AB & C....62 E11
Aghalee L & C....62 E11
Aghaloora Cavan....45 M7
Aghamore Leitrm....44 D6
Aghamore Mayo....42 G7
Aghavannagh Wicklw....31 J8
Agher Meath....38 F5
Aghnagraigue Laois....29 K8
Aglish Tippry....27 M6
Aglish Watfd.... 7 K3
Aglish/An Eaglais Kerry.... 8 G5
Ahafona Kerry....16 E7
Ahanageely Bridge
Galway....27 K2
Ahane Limrck....18 H4
Ahascragh/Áth Eascrach
Galway....35 N7
Ahiohill/Achadh Eochaille
Cork.... 5 J6
Aghohill E Antr....62 C3
Aillwee Cave Clare....25 K5
Ailt an Chorráin/Burtonport
Donegl....64 C11
Aldergrove A & N....62 E8
Allen Kildre....38 E10
Allenwood Kildre....38 E9
Allihies/Na hAilichí Cork.... 2 G7
Anagaire/Annagary
Donegl....64 D10
An Baile Mór/Ballymore
Kerry.... 8 E6
An Baile Thíos/
Ballyhees Galway....24 E5
An Bun Beag/Bunbeg
Donegl....64 E9
An Caiseal/Cashel
Donegl....58 B7
An Caiseal/Cashel Mayo....40 F4
An Carn Mór/Carnmore
Galway....34 G9
An Charraig/Carrick
Donegl....58 C8
An Cheathrú Rua/
Carraroe Galway....33 K10
An Chlais/Clash Kerry.... 8 E3
An Chlochbhuaile/
Cloghbolie Donegl....58 H2
An Chorrchloch/Corclogh
Mayo....48 E6
An Clochán/Cloghan
Donegl....59 M4
An Clochán/Cloghane
Kerry.... 8 G3
An Clochán Liath/Dunglow/
Dungloe Donegl....64 D11
An Daingean/Daingean Uí
Chúis/Dingle Kerry.... 8 E5
An Dúchoraidh/
Doocharry Donegl....59 J2
An Eachléim/Anghleam
Mayo....48 D9
An Eaglais/Aglish Kerry.... 8 G5
An Fál Carrach/Falcarragh
Donegl....64 G7
An Fhairche/Clonbur
Galway....33 N3
An Fód Dubh/Blacksod
Mayo....48 D10

Anghleam/An Eachléim
Mayo....48 D9
An Mhuiríoch/Murreagh
Kerry.... 8 D4
Annacarty Tippry....19 N6
Annaclone AB & C....56 F5
Annacloy NM & D....57 L4
Annacurragh Wicklw....31 K10
Annagary/Anagaire
Donegl....64 D10
Annagassan Louth....47 L6
Annagh Cross Galway....34 G6
Annahilt L & C....56 H2
Annalong NM & D....57 K10
Annalore/Áth an Lobhair
Monhan....54 G8
Annascaul/Abhainn an Scáil
Kerry.... 8 H5
Annayalla Monhan....55 M9
Annestown Watfd....14 B9
Ann Mount Dublin....39 L10
Annsborough NM & D....57 K6
An Rinn/Ring Watfd.... 7 N4
An Spidéal/Spiddal
Galway....33 P10
An tEaden Anfach/
Edenfinfreagh Donegl....59 J5
An Tearmann/Termon
Donegl....65 L9
An tOileán Mór/Bere or
Bear Island Cork.... 3 K8
Antrim A & N....62 E6
An tSraith/Srah Mayo....48 F8
Araglin Tippry....12 F7
Árainn Mhór/Arranmore/
Aran Island Donegl....64 B10
Aran Islands/Oileáin
Árann Galway....24 B4
Ardacluggin Cork.... 2 H7
Ardagh Cork.... 3 K8
Ardagh Meath....46 F5
Ardagh/Ardach Limrck....17 N8
Ardagh/Ardach Longfd....44 H11
Ardamadane Cork....11 P10
Ardara/Ard an Rátha
Donegl....58 F5
Ardattin/Ard Aitinn
Carlow....22 F2
Ardbear Galway....32 E5
Ardboe M Ulst....62 B8
Ardclough Kildre....39 J9
Ardcrony Tippry....27 L8
Ardee/Baile Átha Fhirdhia
Louth....47 J6
Ardfert/Ard Fhearta Kerry....16 C11
Ardfinnan/Ard Fhionáin
Tippry....13 J5
Ardgehane Cork.... 5 K9
Ardglass Cork.... 6 E5
Ardglass NM & D....57 P6
Ardgroom/Dhá Dhrom
Cork.... 3 J5
Ardmore/Aird Mhór Watfd.... 7 L6
Ardnacrusha Clare....18 F3
Ardough Mayo....50 E10
Ardpatrick/Ard Pádraig
Limrck....18 G11
Ardrahan/Ard Raithin
Galway....26 C3
Ardress AB & C....55 Q2
Ardrumkilla Galway....34 E4
Ardsillish Bridge Wicklw....30 J8
Ards Peninsula A & ND....63 Q10
Ardstraw D & S....60 C6
Ardtanagh AB & C....56 H4
Arigna Roscom....53 J11
Arklow/An tInbhear Mór
Wicklw....31 M11
Armagh AB & C....55 P4
Armaghbrague AB & C....55 P7
Armoy CC & G....67 N8
Arney F & O....53 Q6
Arranmore/Aran Island/
Árainn Mhór Donegl....64 B10
Arthurstown Wexfd....14 D7
Articlave CC & G....67 K7
Artigarvan D & S....60 D3
Arvagh/Ármhach Cavan....45 J3
Ashbourne/Cill Dhéagláin
Meath....39 L4
Ashfield AB & C....56 K7
Ashfield F & O....53 F3
Ashford Limrck....17 N11
Ashford/Áth na Fuinseoige
Wicklw....31 L9
Askamore Wexfd....23 J4
Askanagap Wicklw....31 J9

Askeaton/Eas Géitine
Limrck....17 P5
Athboy/Baile Átha Buí
Meath....38 D2
Athea/Áth an tSléibhe
Limrck....17 K8
Athenry/Baile Átha an Rí
Galway....34 H9
Athgarvan Kildre....30 D3
Athlacca Limrck....18 F9
Athleague/Áth Liag
Roscom....35 P3
Athlone/Baile Átha
Luain Wmeath....36 D6
Athlone Services Wmeath....36 F7
Athy Kildre....29 N7
Attanagh Laois....28 H10
Attical NM & D....56 H10
Attipierce Galway....26 G5
Attymass/Áth Tí an
Mheasaigh Mayo....42 C2
Attymon Galway....35 J9
Aughacasla Kerry.... 9 K3
Aughafatten E Antr....62 G2
Aughagower Mayo....41 M8
Augher M Ulst....54 H3
Aughnacliffe/Achadh na
Cloiche Longfd....45 J7
Aughnacloy M Ulst....55 K3
Aughnagurgan AB & C....55 P8
Aughrim Clare....25 N6
Aughrim/Eachroim
Galway....35 N9
Aughrim/Eachroim
Wicklw....31 K10
Aviva Stadium C Dubl....39 N8
Avoca/Abhóca Wicklw....31 M10

B

Baconstown Meath....38 E6
Bagenalstown/Muine Bheag
Carlow....22 C3
Baile an Fheirtéaraigh/
Ballyferriter Kerry.... 8 D5
Baile an Mhuilinn/
Milltown Kerry.... 8 E5
Baile an Sceilg/
Ballinskelligs Kerry.... 2 D3
Baile Bhuirne/
Ballyvourney Cork....10 E10
Baile Chláir/
Claregalway Galway....34 E8
Baile Ghib/Gibbstown
Meath....46 F10
Baile Mhic Íre/
Ballymakeery Cork....10 F10
Baile na Finne/Fintown
Donegl....59 K3
Baile na hAbhann/
Ballinahown Galway....33 L10
Baile na nGall/
Ballynaghall Kerry.... 8 D4
Baile Órthaí/Oristown
Meath....46 E9
Bailieborough/Coill an
Chollaigh Cavan....46 C5
Balbriggan/Baile Brigín
Dublin....39 P2
Baldwinstown Wexfd....15 M6
Balla Mayo....42 C8
Ballacolla Laois....28 G9
Ballagh Tippry....19 Q6
Ballaghaderreen/Bealach
an Doirín Roscom....43 K6
Ballaghboy Clare....25 N10
Ballaghderg Donegl....65 M10
Ballaghkeen Wexfd....23 K8
Ballaghmore Laois....28 D7
Ballapousta Louth....46 H7
Ballina Tippry....26 H11
Ballina/Béal an Átha Mayo....50 E10
Ballinaclash Wicklw....31 L8
Ballinacourty Limrck....18 H3
Ballinacurra Cork.... 5 M4
Ballinafad/Béal an Átha
Fada Sligo....43 N3
Ballinagall Monhan....45 L5
Ballinar Offaly....37 M10
Ballinagh/Béal Átha na
nEach Cavan....45 L5
Ballinahinch Tippry....19 J2
Ballinahown/Baile na
hAbhann Galway....33 L10

Ballinakill/Baile na Coille
Laois....29 J9
Ballinalack Wmeath....37 L2
Ballinalee/Béal Átha na
Lao Longfd....44 H8
Ballinamallard F & O....54 B3
Ballinameen Roscom....43 P6
Ballinamore/Béal an Átha
Móir Leitrm....44 F2
Ballinamore Bridge
Galway....35 N5
Ballinamuck Longfd....44 G6
Ballinamult Watfd....13 L7
Ballinascarty/Béal na
Scairte Cork.... 5 K7
Ballinaslea Mayo....42 B3
Ballinasloe/Béal Átha na
Sluaighe Galway....35 Q8
Ballinbay Bridge Louth....47 J2
Ballinclea Wicklw....31 N9
Ballincollig/Baile an
Chollaigh Cork.... 5 N2
Ballindaggan Wexfd....22 F6
Ballinderreen/Baile an
Doirín Galway....25 N2
Ballinderry Tippry....27 L6
Ballindine/Baile an Daighin
Mayo....42 E11
Ballindrait Donegl....60 C4
Ballinea Wmeath....37 L4
Ballineen/Béal Átha Fhínín
Cork.... 4 H6
Ballingarrane Limrck....17 Q7
Ballingarry Tippry....27 N6
Ballingarry/Baile an Gharraí
Limrck....18 C8
Ballingarry/Baile an Gharraí
Tippry....20 H6
Ballingeary/Béal Átha an
Ghaorthaidh Cork.... 4 E3
Ballinhassig Cork.... 5 P4
Ballinlough Galway....26 H5
Ballinlough Meath....45 Q10
Ballinlough Roscom....43 J9
Ballinphunta Sligo....51 N5
Ballinrobe/Baile an Róba
Mayo....33 Q2
Ballinruan Clare....25 P8
Ballinskelligs/Baile an Sceilg
Kerry.... 2 D3
Ballinspittle/Béal Átha an
Spidéil Cork.... 5 N7
Ballintlea Bridge/Droichead
Bhaile an tSléibhe Watfd.... 7 M5
Ballintober Roscom....43 M10
Ballintogher/Baile an
Tóchair Sligo....52 F8
Ballintoy CC & G....67 Q5
Ballintra/Baile an tSratha
Donegl....59 K10
Ballintubber Mayo....41 P9
Ballinunty Tippry....20 F6
Ballinure Galway....35 P9
Ballitore/Béal Átha an Tuair
Kildre....30 C6
Ballivor/Baile Íomhair
Meath....38 C4
Ballon/Ballán Carlow....22 E2
Balloo AB & ND....63 M11
Ballsmill NM & D....56 M11
Ballyagran Limrck....18 D10
Ballyallaght CC & G....67 P5
Ballybarnes A & ND....63 M8
Ballybay/Béal Átha na
Beithe Monhan....55 L9
Ballyboden Dublin....39 M9
Ballybofey/Bealach Féich
Donegl....59 P5
Ballybogey CC & G....67 N7
Ballyboggan Galway....35 M8
Ballyboughal/Baile Bachaille
Dublin....39 M4
Ballyboy Offaly....28 D3
Ballybrittas Laois....29 L4
Ballybrophy Laois....28 E9
Ballybunion/Baile an
Bhuinneánaigh Kerry....16 E7
Ballycanew/Baile Uí
Chonnmhaí Wexfd....23 L5
Ballycarney Wexfd....22 H6
Ballycarry E Antr....63 L5
Ballycastle CC & G....68 C5
Ballycastle/Baile an Chaisil
Mayo....49 P6
Ballyclare A & N....62 H5
Ballyclerahan Tippry....20 E10

Ballyclogh/ *Baile Cloch*
  Cork 11 L5
Ballycloghan Longfd..... 44 G11
Ballycommon Offaly 37 M9
Ballycommon Tippry 27 K9
Ballyconneely/ *Baile*
  Conaola Galway......32 D6
Ballyconnell/ *Béal Átha*
  Conaill Cavan......54 B10
Ballycotton/ *Baile Choitín*
  Cork 6 G9
Ballycrighan Clare......25 P10
Ballycrossaun Galway......27 L3
Ballycroy Mayo......40 H3
Ballycroy National Park
  Mayo......49 K11
Ballycullane Wexfd......14 H6
Ballycumber/ *Béal Átha*
  Chomair Offaly 36 H8
Ballydehob/ *Béal an dá Chab*
  Cork 3 Q9
Ballydesmond/ *Baile*
  Deasumhan Cork......10 E5
Ballydonegan Cork......2 G8
Ballyduff Wexfd 23 J5
Ballyduff/ *An Baile Dubh*
  Kerry 16 E8
Ballyduff/ *An Baile Dubh*
  Watfd 12 G9
Ballyeaston A & N......62 H5
Ballyedmond Wexfd......23 L7
Ballyfad Wexfd 23 M2
Ballyfarnan/ *Béal Átha*
  Fearnáin Roscom......52 H11
Ballyferriter/ *Baile an*
  Fheirtéaraigh Kerry......8 D5
Ballyfin Laois......28 G5
Ballyforan/ *Béal Átha*
  Feorainne Roscom......35 P5
Ballyfoyle/ *Baile Phóill*
  Kilken 21 M3
Ballygally E Antr 63 K2
Ballygar/ *Béal Átha Ghártha*
  Galway 35 N4
Ballygarrett/ *Baile Ghearóid*
  Wexfd......23 M6
Ballygarvan/ *Baile Garbháin*
  Cork 5 Q4
Ballygawley M Ulst......55 J2
Ballygawley/ *Baile Uí*
  Dhálaigh Sligo 52 L8
Ballygibbon Cork......6 G6
Ballyglass Mayo......42 B9
Ballyglass Mayo......43 J6
Ballygobban Bridge
  Wicklw......31 J8
Ballygowan A & ND......63 L11
Ballygowan Lower
  Galway......26 H5
Ballyguyroe Cork......11 Q3
Ballyhack Wexfd......14 G6
Ballyhahill Limrck......17 L6
Ballyhaise/ *Béal Átha hÉis*
  Cavan 45 M2
Ballyhalbert A & ND 63 Q11
Ballyhale/ *Baile Héil* Kilken......21 M8
Ballyhaunis/ *Béal Átha*
  hAmhnais Mayo......42 G9
Ballyhea Cork......11 M2
Ballyhean Mayo......41 P8
Ballyheelan Cavan......45 M7
Ballyhees/ *An Baile Thíos*
  Galway 24 E5
Ballyheige/ *Baile Uí Thaidhg*
  Kerry......16 C10
Ballyhooly/ *An Baile Átha*
  hUlla Cork 12 B9
Ballyhornan NM & D......57 P5
Ballyjamesduff/ *Baile*
  Shéamais Dhuibh Cavan......45 P6
Ballykelly CC & G......66 G9
Ballykelly Clare......26 D11
Ballyknockan Wicklw......30 H4
Ballykockan Beg Wicklw......31 N6
Ballylanders Cork......6 F9
Ballylanders/ *Baile an*
  Londraigh Limrck......12 C4
Ballylaneen Watfd......13 R8
Ballyleague Roscom......44 D11
Ballylesson L & C......63 J10
Ballylevin Donegl......65 P10
Ballylickey Cork......4 B6
Ballyliffin/ *Baile Lifín*
  Donegl......66 B4
Ballylongford/ *Béal Átha*
  Longfoirt Kerry......16 H7

Ballylooby Tippry......12 H5
Ballylumford E Antr......63 L3
Ballylynan/ *Baile Uí*
  Laigheanáin Laois......29 M8
Ballymacarbry Watfd......13 L6
Ballymacoda Cork......6 H7
Ballymaddock Cross
  Laois......29 L6
Ballymadun Dublin......39 L4
Ballymaghroe Wicklw......31 N6
Ballymagorry D & S......60 D3
Ballymahon/ *Baile Uí*
  Mhatháin Longfd......36 G3
Ballymakeery/ *Baile Mhic*
  Íre Cork......10 F10
Ballymanus Bridge
  Wicklw......31 J9
Ballymartin NM & D......57 J10
Ballymartle Cork......5 P5
Ballymascanlan/ *Baile Mhic*
  Scanláin Louth......47 L2
Ballymena E Antr......62 E3
Ballymoe/ *Béal Átha Mó*
  Galway......43 L10
Ballymoney CC & G......67 N8
Ballymoney Wexfd......23 N3
Ballymore Cork......6 D8
Ballymore Donegl......65 K7
Ballymore/ *An Baile Mór*
  Kerry......8 E6
Ballymore/ *An Baile Mór*
  Wmeath......36 H5
Ballymore Eustace/ *An Baile*
  Mór Kildre......30 F3
Ballymote/ *Baile an Mhóta*
  Sligo......52 D10
Ballymurn Wexfd......23 J9
Ballymurphy/ *Baile Uí*
  Mhurchú Carlow......22 D6
Ballynabola/ *Baile na Buaile*
  Wexfd......14 H4
Ballynabrennagh Lower
  Kerry......9 P2
Ballynacarrigy/ *Baile na*
  Carraige Wmeath......37 K3
Ballynacarrow/ *Baile na Cora*
  Sligo......51 N9
Ballynacorra Cork......6 E7
Ballynacourty Watfd......13 N10
Ballynaghall/ *Baile na nGall*
  Kerry......8 D4
Ballynahinch Kerry......9 P3
Ballynahinch NM & D......57 K3
Ballynahown Wmeath......36 F8
Ballynakilla Cork......3 K8
Ballyneety Limrck......18 G6
Ballynoe/ *An Baile Nua*
  Cork 6 F4
Ballynure A & N......63 J5
Ballyogan/ *Baile Uí Ógain*
  Dublin......39 P10
Ballyorgan Limrck......11 Q2
Ballyouskill/ *Baile Ascaille*
  Kilken......29 J10
Ballypatrick Tippry......13 P3
Ballyporeen/ *Béal Átha*
  Póirín Tippry......12 F6
Ballyragget/ *Béal Átha*
  Ragad Kilken......29 J11
Ballyrashane CC & G......67 M7
Ballyroan/ *Baile Átha an*
  Róine Laois......29 J8
Ballyroe A & N......62 H6
Ballyroe Bridge Kildre......29 P8
Ballyronan M Ulst......61 Q6
Ballysadore/ *Baile Easa*
  Dara Sligo......52 D8
Ballysaggart Watfd......12 H8
Ballyshannon/ *Baile*
  Sonnáin Kildre......30 C5
Ballyshannon/ *Béal Átha*
  Seanaidh Donegl......59 J11
Ballystrudder E Antr......63 M5
Ballyvary/ *Béal Átha*
  Bhearaigh Mayo......42 B6
Ballyvaughan/ *Baile Uí*
  Bheacháin Clare......25 K4
Ballyvourney/ *Baile Bhuirne*
  Cork......10 E10
Ballyvoy CC & G......68 D5
Ballywalter A & ND......63 Q10
Ballyweelin Sligo......52 D6
Ballywilliam Wexfd......23 D9
Balnamore CC & G......67 N8
Balrothery Dublin......39 N2
Balscaddan Dublin......39 N2

Baltimore/ *Dún na Séad*
  Cork 4 B11
Baltinglass/ *Bealach Conglais*
  Wicklw......30 E8
Baltray/ *Baile Trá* Louth......47 M9
Banagher/ *Beannchar*
  Offaly......27 P2
Banbridge AB & C......56 E4
Bandon/ *Droichead na*
  Bandan Cork......5 L5
Bangor A & ND......63 N7
Bangor Abbey A & ND......63 N7
Bangor Erris/ *Baingear*
  Mayo......49 J9
Bankfield Galway......27 N2
Banoge Limrck......18 E8
Bansha/ *An Bháinseach*
  Tippry......19 P9
Banteer/ *Bántir* Cork......11 J6
Bantry/ *Beanntraí* Cork......3 Q7
Bantry House & Garden
  Cork......3 Q7
Barefield Clare......25 N9
Barna Limrck......19 K7
Barna/ *Bearna* Galway......34 B10
Barnahown Tippry......12 F7
Barnatra/ *Barr na Trá* Mayo...48 G7
Barndarrig Wicklw......31 N8
Barntown/ *Baile an*
  Bharúnaigh Wexfd......15 M4
Barraduff Kerry......10 C7
Barr na Trá/ *Barnatra*
  Mayo......48 G7
Barry Longfd......36 G2
Bartlemy Cork......6 D4
Batterjohn Meath......38 G4
Batterstown Meath......39 J5
Bá Uachtair/ *Boyoughter*
  Donegl......58 H3
Bawnard Cork......3 J6
Bawnboy Cavan......53 D10
Bealagrellagh Kerry......9 P3
Béal an Mhuirhead/
  Belmullet Mayo......48 F7
Béal Átha an Ghaorthaidh/
  Ballingeary Cork......4 E3
Bealin Wmeath......36 F6
Bealnablath/ *Béal na Bláth*
  Cork......5 K4
Beara Peninsula Cork......2 G8
Bearna/ *Barna* Galway......34 B10
Beaufort Kerry......9 P7
Bective Abbey Meath......38 G2
Bekan Mayo......42 F9
Belcarra Mayo......41 Q8
Belclare Galway......34 E5
Belcoo F & O......53 M6
Belfast Belfst......63 J9
Belfast International
  Airport A & N......62 H7
Belfast Zoo Belfst......63 J7
Belgooly/ *Béal Guala* Cork......5 Q6
Bellacorick Mayo......49 L10
Bellaghy M Ulst......62 B4
Bellanagare/ *Béal Átha na*
  gCarr Roscom......43 M7
Bellanaleck F & O......53 Q6
Bellanode Monhan......55 J6
Belleek F & O......53 J2
Belleek NM & D......56 B8
Belleek Pottery F & O......53 J2
Belleview Louth......47 M9
Bellewstown Meath......47 L11
Belmayne C Dubl......39 P6
Belmullet/ *Béal an*
  Mhuirmhead Mayo......48 F7
Belturbet/ *Béal Tairbirt*
  Cavan......54 D10
Belvedere House Wmeath...37 M5
Belview Port Kilken......14 F6
Benburb M Ulst......55 N3
Bendooragh CC & G......67 N9
Bennettsbridge/ *Droichead*
  Binéid Kilken......21 N6
Beragh F & O......60 G10
Bere or Bear Island/
  An tOileán Mór Cork......3 K8
Bessbrook NM & D......56 C8
Bettystown/ *Baile an*
  Bhiataigh Meath......47 N10
Bhréanainn/ *Brandon*
  Kerry......8 G2
Bilboa Carlow......29 M11
Birdhill Tippry......19 J2
Birdhill Services Tippry......19 J2
Birr/ *Biorra* Offaly......27 Q4

Birr Castle Gardens &
  Science Centre Offaly......27 Q4
Blackditch/ *An Claí Dubh*
  Wicklw......31 N5
Blacklion/ *An Blaic* Cavan......53 M6
Blackrock C Cork......6 B7
Blackrock Louth......47 L4
Blackrock/ *An Charraig*
  Dhubh Dublin......39 P9
Blacksod/ *An Fód Dubh*
  Mayo......48 D10
Blackwater/ *An Abhainn*
  Dubh Wexfd......23 L9
Blackwatertown AB & C......55 N3
Blanchardstown Dublin......39 L7
Blarney/ *An Bhlarna* Cork......11 P10
Blarney Castle Cork......11 P10
Bleary AB & C......56 D3
Blennerville/ *Cathair Uí*
  Mhóráin Kerry......9 N3
Blessington/ *Baile Coimín*
  Wicklw......30 G3
Blue Ball Offaly......37 J11
Bockagh Roscom......43 K5
Bodyke Clare......26 E9
Bofeenaun Mayo......41 P4
Boherboy/ *Bóthar Buí*
  Kerry......8 D4
Boherbue Cork......10 G5
Boherlahan/ *An Bóthar*
  Leathan Tippry......20 C6
Bohernabreena Dublin......39 L9
Boho F & O......53 N5
Bohola/ *Both Chomhla*
  Mayo......42 D5
Bolea CC & G......67 J8
Boleynass Wicklw......31 M6
Book of Kells C Dubl......39 N8
Boolavogue/ *Baile Mhaodhóg*
  Wexfd......23 K6
Boolybane Cork......4 D10
Borcarnagh Cork......3 P6
Borris/ *An Bhuiríos* Carlow...22 C5
Borris-in-Ossory/
  Buiríos Mór Osraí Laois......28 D8
Borrisokane/ *Buiríos Uí*
  Chéin Tippry......20 M7
Borrisoleigh Tippry......20 B2
Bóthar Buí/ *Boherboy*
  Kerry......8 D4
Boyle/ *Mainistir na Búille*
  Roscom......43 P4
Boyne Valley/ *Brú na Bóinne*
  Meath......47 K10
Boyoughter/ *Bá Uachtair*
  Donegl......58 H3
Boytown Mayo......49 P5
Brandon/ *Bhréanainn*
  Kerry......8 G2
Brandon Mountain/ *Cnoc*
  Bréanainn Kerry......8 F3
Bray/ *Brí* Wicklw......39 Q11
Bready D & S......60 D2
Breaghwy/ *Bréachmhaigh*
  Mayo......41 Q7
Bree/ *Brí* Wexfd......22 G9
Bridebridge Cork......6 D3
Bridge End Donegl......58 G7
Bridgend Donegl......66 B9
Bridgetown Clare......18 G2
Bridgetown Donegl......59 K9
Bridgetown Donegl......65 Q10
Bridgetown/ *Baile an*
  Droichid Wexfd......15 M7
Brinlack/ *Bun na Leaca*
  Donegl......64 E7
Brittas Dublin......39 K10
Broadford Kildre......38 C6
Broadford/ *Áth Leathan*
  Clare......26 E11
Broadford/ *Béal an Átha*
  Limrck......17 P11
Broadway Wexfd......15 Q7
Brookeborough F & O......54 D5
Brooklodge Cork......6 D8
Brookville Tippry......19 M9
Brosna Kerry......10 D2
Brosna Offaly......27 P2
Broughshane E Antr......62 F2
Bruckless/ *An Bhroclais*
  Donegl......58 F8
Bruff/ *An Brú* Limrck......18 G8
Brú na Bóinne/ *Boyne Valley*
  Meath......47 K10
Bruree/ *Brú Rí* Limrck......18 E9
Brusna Roscom......43 J5

Bryansford NM & D.............57 J7
Buckna E Antr.....................62 G2
Bullaun Galway...............35 K10
Buloughera Clare...............17 L3
Bunacurry/ Bun an Churraigh
Mayo...............................40 E4
Bun an Churraigh/
Bunacurry Mayo.............40 E4
Bunbeg/ An Bun Beag
Donegl.............................64 E9
Bunbrosna Wmeath.........37 L2
Bunclody/ Bun Clóidi
Wexfd...............................22 G4
Buncrana/ Bun Cranncha
Donegl.............................65 Q7
Bundoran/ Bun Dobhráin
Donegl.............................52 G2
Bunmahon/ Bun Machan
Watfd...............................14 A9
Bun na hAbhna/
Bunnahown Mayo...........48 G8
Bunnahowen/ Bun na
hAbhna Mayo..................48 G8
Bun na Leaca/ Brinlack
Donegl.............................64 E7
Bunnanaddan/ Bun an
Fhendáin Sligo...............43 K2
Bunnyconnellan Mayo.....50 G10
Bunratty Clare..................18 C3
Bunratty Castle & Folk
Park Clare.......................18 C3
Burke Court Galway.........27 K6
Burke's Cross Laois.........28 F6
Burncourt Tippry..............12 F5
Burnfoot CC & G..............66 H11
Burnfoot/ Bun na hAbhann
Donegl.............................66 B9
Burnside A & N.................62 H5
Burren Mayo.....................41 P5
Burren National Park
Clare...............................25 M6
Burren Perfumery Clare....25 L6
Burtonport/ Ailt an Chorráin
Donegl.............................64 C11
Bushmills CC & G.............67 N5
Butlers Bridge/ Droichead an
Bhuitléaraigh Cavan........45 M2
Butlerstown Cork...............5 L9
Buttevant/ Cill na Mallach
Cork.................................11 M4
Bweeng/ Na Boinn Cork....11 L8

C

Cadamstown Offaly...........28 D4
Caherconlish/ Cathair Chinn
Lis Limrck........................18 H6
Caherdaniel/ Cathair Dónall
Kerry.................................2 F5
Cahergarriff Cork...............2 H8
Caherlistrane Galway.......34 D5
Cahersiveen/ Cathair
Saidhbhín Kerry................8 F10
Cahir/ Án Chathair Tippry...13 J4
Cahore/ Cathóir Wexfd.......23 N6
Caim Wexfd......................22 F7
Caladh Thaidhg Galway....33 K10
Caledon M Ulst.................55 M4
Callan/ Callain Kilken........21 K7
Caltra Galway...................35 M6
Calverstown/ Baile an
Chalbhaigh Kildre.............30 D5
Camaross/ Camross Wexfd ..15 K4
Camlough NM & D...........56 C8
Camolin/ Cam Eolaing
Wexfd...............................23 K5
Camp Kerry.......................9 K4
Campile/ Ceann Poill
Wexfd...............................14 G5
Canningstown Cavan.......46 B4
Cape Clear Island/ Oileán
Chléire Cork.......................3 Q12
Cappagh Cork....................5 P6
Cappagh Beg Clare...........25 N9
Cappagh Bridge Galway....27 J4
Cappagh More Clare..........25 N9
Cappaghmore Roscom......36 D7
Cappagowlaun Galway......32 G2
Cappaleigh South Cork.......3 M7
Cappalusk Galway............35 K7
Cappamore/ An Cheapach
Mhór Limrck.....................19 K5
Cappavilla Clare................18 G4
Cappwhite/ An Cheapach
Tippry...............................19 M5

Cappoquin/ Ceapach Choinn
Watfd...............................13 K9
Carbury Kildre..................38 C8
Cardy A & ND....................63 P9
Cargahdoo Monhan..........55 N11
Cargan E Antr...................68 D10
Carland M Ulst.................61 M10
Carlanstown Meath..........46 E9
Carlingford/ Cairlinn
Louth...............................47 N2
Carlow/ Ceatharlach
Carlow.............................29 P10
Carlow Services Carlow....30 C11
Carna Galway...................32 G8
Carnacon Mayo................41 Q9
Carnalbanagh E Antr........62 H2
Carnaross Meath..............46 C9
Carncastle E Antr.............63 K2
Carndonagh/ Carn
Domhnach Donegl...........66 D5
Carnew/ Carn an Bhua
Wicklw.............................23 J3
Carney/ Fearann Uí
Chearnaigh Sligo.............52 D5
Carnlough E Antr..............68 F10
Carnmore/ An Carn Mór
Galway.............................34 E9
Carnteel M Ulst................55 K3
Carrabane/ An Ceathrú Bán
Galway.............................35 J11
Carracastle Mayo.............42 H4
Carragh Kildre..................38 F10
Carraholly Mayo................41 L7
Carraig Airt/ Carrigart
Donegl.............................65 L6
Carran Clare.....................25 L6
Carraroe/ An Cheathrú Rua
Galway.............................33 K10
Carrauntoohil Kerry...........9 N9
Carrick/ An Charraig
Donegl.............................58 C8
Carrick/ An Charraig
Wexfd...............................15 K6
Carrick-a-Rede Rope
Bridge CC & G..................68 B5
Carrickboy Longfd............36 H2
Carrickbyrne Wexfd..........15 J4
Carrickfergus E Antr.........63 L6
Carrickfergus Castle
E Antr...............................63 L6
Carrickmacross/ Carraig
Mhachaire Rois Monhan...46 F4
Carrickmore F & O............61 J9
Carrick-on-Shannon/ Cora
Droma Rúisc Leitrm..........44 B5
Carrick-on-Suir/ Carraig na
Siúire Tippry....................13 Q4
Carrigagrenane
Crossroads Cork...............4 G8
Carrigaholt Clare..............16 D5
Carrigaline/ Carraig Uí
Leighín Cork......................6 B9
Carrigallen/ Carraig
Aileann Leitrm..................44 H4
Carriganimmy Cork..........10 G9
Carriganore Watfd............14 D6
Carrigans/ An Carraigín
Donegl.............................66 B11
Carrigart/ Carraig Airt
Donegl.............................65 L6
Carrigkerry Limrck............17 M8
Carrigmore Cork................4 H6
Carrignavar Cork..............11 Q9
Carrigrohane Cork.............5 P2
Carrigtwohill/ Carraig
Thuathail Cork...................6 D7
Carrowclare CC & G.........66 G8
Carrowdore A & ND..........63 P9
Carrowkennedy/ Ceathrú
Chinnéide Mayo...............41 L10
Carrowmenagh Donegl......66 F4
Carrowteige/ Ceathrú
Thaidhg Mayo..................48 H5
Carrybridge F & O............54 B6
Carryduff L & C.................63 K10
Cartron More Roscom........43 K6
Casey Donegl....................65 J6
Cashel/ An Caiseal Donegl..58 B7
Cashel/ An Caiseal Mayo...40 F4
Cashel/ Caiseal Tippry......20 C7
Cashel Cross Laois...........29 J7
Cashellahenny Mayo.........43 J6
Cashel Services Tippry.....20 C8
Casla/ Costelloe Galway...33 L9
Castlebaldwin/ Béal Átha na
gCarraigíní Sligo...............52 F11

Castlebar/ Caisleán an
Bharraigh Mayo................41 P6
Castlebellingham/ Baile an
Ghearlánaigh Louth..........47 L5
Castlebellingham Services
Louth...............................47 K5
Castleblakeney/ Gallach
Galway.............................35 L6
Castleblayney/ Baile na
Lorgan Monhan................55 N10
Castlebridge/ Droichead an
Chaisleáin Wexfd.............15 P3
Castlecaulfield M Ulst.......61 M11
Castlecomer/ Caisleán an
Chomair Kilken.................29 K11
Castleconnell/ Caisleán Uí
Chonaill Limrck.................18 H3
Castle Coole F & O...........54 B5
Castlecoote Roscom.........35 P2
Castlecor Cork..................11 L4
Castlecor Meath................45 P8
Castlecove Kerry................2 G4
Castlecuff Cross Laois......28 G3
Castledaly Wmeath...........36 F7
Castledawson M Ulst........61 Q5
Castlederg D & S..............60 B7
Castledermot/ Díseart
Diarmada Kildre...............30 C8
Castledockrell Wexfd........22 G6
Castlefinn/ Caisleán na
Finne Donegl....................60 B4
Castlegregory/ Caisleán
Ghriaire Kerry....................9 J3
Castleisland/ Oileán Ciarraí
Kerry...............................10 B4
Castleknock Dublin..........39 L7
Castle Lambert Galway.....34 G9
Castlelyons/ Caisleán Ó
Liatháin Cork.....................6 D3
Castlemagner Cork...........11 K5
Castlemaine/ Caisleán na
Mainge Kerry.....................9 N5
Castlemartyr/ Baile na Martra
Cork.................................6 G7
Castleplunket Roscom......43 N9
Castlepollard/ Baile na gCros
Wmeath...........................45 N10
Castlerea/ An Caisleán
Riabhach Roscom............43 L9
Castlerock CC & G............67 K6
Castletown Clare..............25 L6
Castletown Cork................4 H5
Castletown Cork................5 Q8
Castletown Limrck............18 C9
Castletown Meath.............46 F8
Castletown Wexfd.............23 N2
Castletown Wmeath.........45 M9
Castletown/ Baile an
Chaisleáin Laois...............28 F7
Castletownbere/ Castletown
Berehaven/Baile Chaisleáin
Bhearra Cork.....................3 J7
Castletown Berehaven/
Castletownbere/Baile
Chaisleáin Bhearra Cork....3 J7
Castletown Geoghegan/
Baile Chaisleáin na
nGeochagán Wmeath.......37 K6
Castletown House
Kildre...............................39 J8
Castletownroche/ Baile
Chaisleáin an Róistigh
Cork.................................11 Q5
Castletownshend/ Baile an
Chaisleáin Laois...............4 E10
Castle Ward NM & D.........57 P4
Castlewarren Kilken..........21 P3
Castlewellan NM & D........57 J6
Castlewellan Forest Park
NM & D.............................57 J6
Castlewood Cross Laois....28 H10
Cathair Dónall/
Caherdaniel Kerry.............2 F5
Causeway/ An Tóchar
Kerry...............................16 D9
Cavan/ An Cabhán Cavan..45 J6
Ceann Trá/ Ventry Kerry......8 D5
Ceathrú Thaidhg/
Carrowteige Mayo............48 H5
Cecilstown Cork................11 L4
Céide Fields Mayo............49 M5
Celbridge/ Cill Droichid
Kildre...............................39 J8
Chapeltown Kerry.............5 D10
Chapeltown NM & D..........57 J6
Charlemont AB & C...........55 P2

Charlestown/ Baile Chathail
Mayo...............................42 G4
Charleville/ Ráth Luirc
Cork.................................18 E11
Cheekpoint/ Pointe na Síge
Watfd...............................14 F6
Chester Beatty Library
C Dubl..............................39 N8
Christ Church Cathedral
C Dubl..............................39 N8
Church Bay CC & G...........68 C3
Church Hill F & O..............53 N2
Churchtown Cork................6 F7
Churchtown Cork................6 F9
Churchtown Donegl..........60 C4
Churchtown Limrck...........17 N9
Churchtown Wexfd............14 G9
Churchtown Wexfd............15 Q7
Churchtown/ Baile an
Teampail Cork..................11 M3
Cill Charthaigh/ Kilcar
Donegl.............................58 D8
Cill Chiaráin/ Kilkieran
Galway.............................32 H8
Cill Rónáin/ Kilronan
Galway.............................24 C4
Cill Ulta/ Killult Donegl.....64 G7
Cionn Caslach/ Kincasslagh
Donegl.............................64 C10
City of Derry Airport
D & S...............................66 E9
Clabby F & O....................54 E3
Claddaghduff Galway.......32 C3
Clady A & N......................62 F7
Clady D & S......................60 B5
Clady M Ulst....................62 B3
Clady Milltown AB & C......56 B6
Clahane Kerry.....................9 N3
Clane/ Claonadh Kildre......38 G9
Clara/ Clóirtheach Offaly...37 J8
Claran Galway..................34 B5
Clare AB & C.....................56 C5
Clarecastle/ Droichead an
Chláir Clare......................25 M11
Claregalway/ Baile Chláir
Galway.............................34 E8
Clare Island Mayo............40 E7
Claremorris/ Clár Chlainne
Mhuiris Mayo...................42 F10
Clarina Limrck..................18 E5
Clarinbridge/ Droichead an
Chláirín Galway...............34 F10
Clash/ An Chlais Kerry.......8 E3
Clash Cross Laois............28 G8
Clashmore/ Clais Mhór
Watfd.................................7 K5
Classes Lake Cork.............5 N2
Claudy D & S....................60 G2
Cleggan/ An Cloigeann
Galway.............................32 D3
Cleristown Wexfd..............15 M6
Clifden/ An Clochán
Galway.............................32 E4
Cliffoney/ Cliafuine Sligo...52 E2
Cliffs of Moher Clare.........24 F7
Clogagh Cork.....................5 N8
Clogh E Antr.....................68 B11
Clogh Laois......................28 F9
Clogh/ An Chloch Kilken....29 L10
Cloghan Wmeath..............37 P3
Cloghan/ An Clochán
Donegl.............................59 M4
Cloghan/ An Clochán
Offaly...............................36 E11
Cloghane/ An Clochán
Kerry.................................8 G3
Cloghbolie/ An Chlochbhuaile
Donegl.............................58 H2
Clogheen/ An Chloichín
Tippry...............................12 H6
Clogher M Ulst.................54 G3
Clogher Mayo...................41 M7
Clogher Mayo...................41 Q9
Clogher Roscom...............50 J6
Clogherane Kerry...............3 L5
Clogherhead/ Ceann
Chlochair Louth................47 N8
Clogh Mills CC & G...........68 B10
Cloghreo/ Cloch Reo
Cork.................................11 N11
Clohamon/ Cloch Ámainn
Wexfd...............................22 G5
Clologe/ Cloch Cúirte
Wexfd...............................23 K5
Clonaghadoo Laois..........28 H3
Clonakenny Tippry............28 B9

Clonakilty/ *Cloich na Coillte*
Cork 5 J8
Clonalis House Roscom 43 L8
Clonard Meath 38 B5
Clonaslee/ *Cluain na Slí*
Laois 28 F3
Clonbulloge/ *Cluain Bolg*
Offaly 38 B10
Clonbur/ *An Fhairche*
Galway 33 N3
Clondalkin Dublin 39 L8
Clondrohid/ *Cluain*
Droichead Cork 10 G10
Clondulane Cork 12 D9
Clonea Watfd 13 Q6
Clonee Meath 39 K6
Cloneen Tippry 20 G8
Clonegall/ *Cluain na nGall*
Carlow 22 G3
Clonenagh Cross Laois ... 28 G6
Clones/ *Cluain Eois*
Monhan 54 G8
Clongeen Wexfd 15 J5
Clonglaskan Cork 2 H8
Clonigulane Clare 17 K2
Clonlara/ *Cluain Lára*
Clare 18 G3
Clonmacnoise/ *Cluain Mnic*
Nóis Offaly 36 D8
Clonmacnoise Monastic
Site Offaly 36 D8
Clonmany/ *Cluain Maine*
Donegl 66 B4
Clonmel/ *Cluain Meala*
Tippry 13 M4
Clonmellon/ *Ráistín*
Wmeath 46 C11
Clonmore Carlow 30 G10
Clonmore Louth 47 M7
Clonoghil Cross Laois 28 E7
Clonoulty Tippry 20 B5
Clonroche/ *Cluain an*
Róistigh Wexfd 22 F9
Clonsilla Dublin 39 L7
Clontarf C Dubl 39 P7
Clontibret Monhan 55 M8
Clontubrid Kilken 21 K2
Clonvaraghan NM & D 57 J5
Clonygowan/ *Cluain na*
nGamhan Offaly 29 J2
Cloonagh Galway 32 F2
Cloonbeggaun Roscom 26 C8
Cloondara/ *Cluain Dá Ráth*
Longfd 44 E9
Clooney Clare 25 P10
Cloonfad/ *Cluain Fada*
Roscom 42 H10
Cloonfada Clare 26 G11
Clooniff Roscom 36 C8
Cloonkeen Kerry 10 D9
Cloonkeevy/ *Cluain*
Ciabhaigh Sligo 51 N11
Cloonnagro Clare 26 D7
Cloontuskert Roscom 44 C10
Clough NM & D 57 L5
Clough/ *An Chloch* Wexfd .. 23 L4
Cloughjordan/ *Cloch*
Shiurdáin Tippry 27 N8
Cloyne/ *Cluain* Cork 6 F8
Clydagh Cork 3 L7
Cnocán na Líne/
Knocknalina Mayo 48 G6
Cnoc Bréanainn/ *Brandon*
Mountain Kerry 8 F3
Coachford/ *Áth an Chóiste*
Cork 11 L11
Coagh M Ulst 61 P8
Coalisland M Ulst 61 N10
Cobh/ *An Cóbh* Cork 6 C8
Colehill Longfd 36 H2
Coleraine CC & G 67 L7
Colliga Wicklw 30 G7
Collinstown/ *Baile na*
gCailleach Wmeath 45 P11
Collon/ *Collann* Louth 47 J8
Collooney/ *Cúil Mhuine*
Sligo 52 D8
Comber A & ND 63 M10
Common Bridge Donegl ... 58 F6
Conahy Kilken 21 L2
Cong/ *Conga* Mayo 33 P3
Conlig A & ND 63 M8
Conna Cork 12 F10
Connemara National Park
Galway 32 F3
Connor E Antr 62 F4

Convoy/ *Conmhaigh*
Donegl 59 R3
Coogue Mayo 42 F8
Cookstown M Ulst 61 N8
Coolaney/ *Cúil Áine* Sligo .. 51 N8
Coolboy Donegl 65 M10
Coolboy Wicklw 23 J2
Coolcap Cork 6 G6
Coolcoosaun Clare 26 F8
Coolderry Offaly 28 B6
Coole/ *An Chúil* Wmeath .. 26 H9
Coole/ *An Chúil* Wmeath .. 45 M10
Coolea/ *Cúil Aodha* Cork .. 10 E10
Coole-Garryland Nature
Reserve Galway 25 P5
Coolfadda Galway 35 L10
Coolgreany/ *Cúil Ghréine*
Wexfd 23 M2
Coolick Kerry 9 R6
Coolieragh Cork 3 P6
Coolmore Cross Cork 6 C9
Coolnagun Wmeath 45 L10
Coolnasmear Watfd 13 M9
Coolrain Cross Laois 28 E7
Coolyslin Lower Donegl ... 60 B5
Coolyslin Upper Donegl ... 60 B5
Coon/ *Coan* Kilken 29 L11
Coonnaluinga Galway 32 G2
Cooraclare/ *Cuar an Chláir*
Clare 16 H3
Coosane Tippry 18 H2
Cootehall Roscom 43 Q4
Cootehill/ *Muinchille*
Cavan 54 H11
Coppeen Cork 4 H4
Copperalley Cork 7 J6
Corbally Cross Laois 28 H8
Corbet AB & C 56 F5
Corclogh/ *An Chorrchloch*
Mayo 48 E6
Cordal Kerry 10 C4
Cork/ *Corcaigh* C Cork 5 Q2
Cork Airport Cork 5 Q3
Corkey CC & G 68 B9
Corkley AB & C 55 P7
Corlismore Cavan 45 K5
Cornafean Cavan 45 K5
Cornamona/ *Corr na Móna*
Galway 33 M4
Cornelscourt Dublin 39 P9
Corofin/ *Cora Finne* Clare .. 25 L8
Corrandromaun
Crossroads Watfd 6 H4
Corrandulla Galway 34 D7
Correen E Antr 62 E2
Corr na Móna/ *Cornamona*
Galway 33 M4
Corrofin Galway 34 F6
Costelloe/ *Casla* Galway .. 33 L9
Courtbrack Cork 11 N10
Courtmacsherry/ *Cúirt Mhic*
Shéafraidh Cork 5 M8
Courtmacuddy Watfd 22 F8
Courtown/ *Baile na Cúirte*
Wexfd 23 M4
Courtstown Cork 6 C7
Coynes Cross Services
Wicklw 31 N5
Craanford Wexfd 23 K3
Craggaunowen Project
Clare 26 C11
Craigavole CC & G 67 M11
Craigavon AB & C 56 C2
Craigywarren E Antr 62 E2
Cranagh D & S 60 H5
Cratloe Clare 18 D3
Craughwell/ *Creachmhaoil*
Galway 34 H10
Crawford Art Gallery
Cork 5 Q2
Crawfordsburn A & ND 63 M7
Creagh Cork 4 C10
Creagh/ *An Chríoch*
Galway 35 Q8
Creagh/ *An Chríoch* Clare .. 16 H2
Creeslough/ *An Craoslach*
Donegl 65 K7
Creevy Donegl 58 H11
Creggan NM & D 55 Q10
Creggs Galway 35 P3
Crettyard Laois 29 L10
Crinkill Offaly 27 Q5
Croagh Limrck 18 C7
Croboy Meath 38 B5
Croghan Offaly 37 N8

Croithlí/ *Crolly* Donegl 64 E10
Croke Park/ *Páirc an*
Chrócaigh C Dubl 39 N7
Crolly/ *Croithlí* Donegl 64 E10
Cromane/ *An Cromán*
Kerry 9 K6
Cronagort Clare 24 G6
Crooke/ *An Crúc* Watfd ... 14 G7
Crookedwood/ *Tigh Munna*
Wmeath 37 N2
Crookedwood Cross
Laois 28 G9
Crookhaven/ *An Cruachán*
Cork 3 M11
Crookstown Cork 5 K3
Crookstown Kildre 30 D6
Croom/ *Cromadh* Limrck .. 18 E7
Crosreagh Cork 5 L7
Cross Mayo 33 Q3
Crossabeg Wexfd 15 N3
Crossakeel/ *Crosa Caoil*
Meath 46 B10
Crossbarry/ *Crois an*
Bharraigh Cork 5 N4
Cross Bridge Wicklw 30 H10
Crossdoney Cavan 45 L4
Crossgar NM & D 57 M3
Crosshaven/ *Bun an*
Tábhairne Cork 6 C9
Crosskeys Cavan 45 N5
Crossmaglen NM & D 55 Q10
Crossmolina/ *Crois*
Mhaoilíona Mayo 50 C10
Crossnacole Bridge
Wicklw 30 F9
Crossnacreevy L & C 63 K10
Crumlin A & N 62 F8
Crusheen/ *Croisín* Clare .. 25 N8
Crushoa Galway 25 N3
Cuckel's Crossroads
Kildre 30 C6
Cuddagh Cross Laois 28 F8
Cúil Aodha/ *Coolea* Cork .. 10 E10
Culdaff/ *Cúil Dabhcha*
Donegl 66 E4
Cullahill Laois 28 G11
Cullaville NM & D 55 P11
Cullen Tippry 19 L2
Cullenstown/ *Baile Uí*
Choileáin Wexfd 15 K7
Cullybackey E Antr 62 D2
Cullyfad Longfd 44 G9
Cullyhanna NM & D 55 Q9
Culmore D & S 60 F10
Culmullin Meath 38 H5
Curracloe Watfd 23 K10
Curragha Meath 39 K3
Curraghavoe Cork 12 E6
Curraghboy Roscom 36 B5
Curraghmore Cork 12 E6
Curragh Racecourse
Kildre 30 C3
Curran M Ulst 62 D3
Curry/ *An Choraidh* Sligo .. 42 G3
Cushendall CC & G 68 E7
Cushendun CC & G 68 E7
Cut Bush Kildre 30 C4

D

Daingean/ *An Daingean*
Offaly 37 N9
Daingean Uí Chúis/ *An*
Daingean/Dingle Kerry 8 E5
Dalkey/ *Deilginis* Dublin ... 39 Q9
Daly's Cross/ *Crosaire Uí*
Dhálaigh Limrck 18 H3
Darkley AB & C 55 P7
Darragh Limrck 12 B5
Darragh Cross NM & D 57 M2
Darver Louth 47 K5
Davidstown Wexfd 22 G8
Dawros Kerry 3 N3
Delgany/ *Deilgne* Wicklw .. 31 N3
Delvin/ *Dealbhna* Wmeath .. 38 B2
Deputy's Pass Wicklw 31 M7
Dernacartha Roscom 43 K7
Dernaflaw CC & G 61 K2
Derragh Cross Laois 28 G6
Derreentaggart Cork 3 J2
Derrinturn Kildre 38 D8
Derry/ *Londonderry* D & S .. 66 C10
Derrybeg/ *Doirí Beaga*
Donegl 64 E8
Derryboye NM & D 57 M2

Derrybrien Galway 26 E5
Derrygonnelly F & O 53 N3
Derryhaun Longfd 36 E2
Derryheena Clare 25 P8
Derrykearn Cross Laois ... 28 H8
Derrykeighan CC & G 67 P7
Derryleigh Bridge Cork 4 E9
Derrylin F & O 54 B8
Derrymacash AB & C 56 C2
Derrymore Kerry 8 G10
Derry Walls D & S 66 C10
Dervock CC & G 67 P7
Desertmartin M Ulst 61 P5
Dickeystown A & N 62 H5
Dingle/ *An Daingean/Daingean*
Uí Chúis Kerry 8 E5
Dingle Oceanworld Kerry .. 8 E5
Doagh A & N 62 H6
Doirí Beaga/ *Derrybeg*
Donegl 64 E8
Dolla Tippry 27 L11
Dollingstown AB & C 56 E2
Domhnach Phádraig/
Donaghpatrick Meath 46 F10
Donabate/ *Domhnach Bat*
Dublin 39 P4
Donacarney Meath 47 M10
Donagh F & O 54 D8
Donaghadee A & ND 63 P8
Donaghcloney AB & C 56 E3
Donaghmore Laois 28 E9
Donaghmore M Ulst 61 M10
Donaghmore Meath 39 L4
Donaghmore Meath 46 G10
Donaghpatrick/ *Domhnach*
Phádraig Meath 46 F10
Donard/ *Dún Ard* Wicklw .. 30 F6
Donaskeagh Tippry 19 N7
Donegal/ *Dún na nGall*
Donegl 59 K8
Donegal Airport/
Aerfort Dhún na nGall
Donegl 64 D9
Donemana/ *Dunnamanagh*
D & S 60 E3
Doneraile/ *Dún ar Aill*
Cork 11 P4
Doneraile Wildlife Park
Cork 11 P4
Donohill Tippry 19 N7
Donore Kildre 38 F10
Donore Meath 47 K10
Donoughmore Cork 11 L9
Dooagh Mayo 40 D4
Doocharry/ *An Dúchoraidh*
Donegl 59 J2
Doody Limrck 17 N10
Dooega/ *Dumha Éige*
Mayo 40 E5
Doogary Roscom 43 K5
Doohamlet Monhan 55 M9
Doohat Bridge Monhan 54 H9
Doohooma/ *Dumha Thuama*
Mayo 48 F10
Doolin/ *Dúlainn* Clare 24 G6
Doon Galway 35 M7
Doon Offaly 36 F8
Doon/ *Dún* Limrck 19 L5
Doonbeg Clare 16 G2
Dooneen Clare 25 N10
Dooniver/ *Dún Ibhir*
Mayo 40 F3
Dooyork/ *Dumha Dhearc*
Mayo 48 F10
Douglas Cork 6 B8
Douglas Bridge D & S 60 D5
Downey's Bridge Cork 11 L9
Downhill Demesne
& Hezlett House
CC & G 67 K6
Downings/ *Na Dúnaibh*
Donegl 65 K6
Downpatrick NM & D 57 M5
Dowra Leitrm 53 K8
Doyle's Cross Laois 29 L9
Drains Bay E Antr 63 K2
Drangan/ *Drongán* Tippry .. 20 G7
Draperstown M Ulst 61 M5
Drimoleague/ *Drom dhá Liag*
Cork 4 D7
Dripsey Cork 11 L11
Drogheda/ *Droichead Átha*
Louth 47 L9
Droichead Bhaile an
tSléibhe/ *Ballintlea*
Bridge Watfd 7 M5

Droim Loch Druid/
Drumlaghdrid Donegl..........58 G2
Drom Tippry..........20 C2
Dromahair/ *Droim Dhá*
Thair Leitrm..........52 G7
Dromara L & C..........56 H4
Drombane Kerry..........3 N4
Dromcollogher/ *Drom*
Collachair Limrck..........18 B11
Dromina/ *Drom Aidhne*
Cork..........11 L2
Dromineer Tippry..........27 K8
Dromiskin Louth..........47 L5
Dromkeen Limrck..........19 J6
Drommahane Cork..........11 M6
Drommartin Kerry..........16 D9
Dromod/ *Dromad* Leitrm..........44 E7
Dromore AB & C..........56 G3
Dromore F & O..........60 C11
Dromore West Sligo..........51 J7
Drumahoe D & S..........66 D10
Drumaness NM & D..........57 K4
Drumaroad NM & D..........57 K5
Drumbane Tippry..........19 Q4
Drumbeg L & C..........63 J10
Drumbo L & C..........63 J10
Drumcliff/ *Droim Chliabh*
Sligo..........52 D5
Drumcondra/ *Droim Conrach*
Meath..........46 G7
Drumcree Wmeath..........45 Q11
Drumdangan Wicklw..........31 M7
Drumfries/ *Droim Fraoigh*
Donegl..........66 B6
Drumgarra Monhan..........55 M10
Drumkeen Donegl..........59 Q3
Drumkeeran/ *Droim*
Caorthainn Leitrm..........53 J9
Drumkilly Cavan..........45 M6
Drumlaghdrid/ *Droim Loch*
Druid Donegl..........58 G2
Drumlish/ *Droim Lis*
Longfd..........44 G7
Drumquin F & O..........60 C9
Drumrath Cavan..........45 M6
Drumree Meath..........38 H4
Drumshallon Louth..........47 L8
Drumshanbo/ *Droim*
Seanbhó Leitrm..........44 C2
Drumsna/ *Droim ar Snámh*
Leitrm..........44 C5
Drumsurn CC & G..........67 J10
Drung Cavan..........45 P2
Duagh/ *Dubháth* Kerry..........17 J9
Dualla Tippry..........20 D7
Dublin/ *Baile Átha Cliath*
C Dubl..........39 N8
Dublin Airport Dublin..........39 N6
Dublin Castle C Dubl..........39 N8
Dublin City Gallery,
The Hugh Lane C Dubl..........39 N7
Dublin Zoo C Dubl..........39 M7
Duggan's Hill Galway..........27 J4
Dugort Mayo..........40 E3
Duleek/ *Damhliag* Meath..........47 K11
Dumha Dhearc/ *Dooyork*
Mayo..........48 F10
Dumha Éige/ *Dooega*
Mayo..........40 E5
Dumha Thuama/
Doohooma Mayo..........48 F10
Dunabrattin/ *Dún an*
Bhratain Watfd..........14 B9
Dunadry A & N..........62 F6
Dún Aonghasa Galway..........24 B4
Dunbell Kilken..........21 N5
Dunboyne/ *Dún Búinne*
Meath..........39 K6
Duncannon/ *Dún Canann*
Wexfd..........14 G7
Dún Chaoin/ *Dunquin*
Kerry..........8 C5
Duncormick/ *Dun Cormaic*
Wexfd..........15 L7
Dundalk/ *Dún Dealgan*
Louth..........47 K3
Dunderrow Cork..........5 N6
Dunderry Meath..........38 F2
Dundonald L & C..........63 L9
Dundrod L & C..........62 G8
Dundrum Dublin..........39 N9
Dundrum NM & D..........57 L6
Dundrum Tippry..........19 P6
Dunfanaghy/ *Dún*
Fionnachaidh Donegl..........65 J4
Dungannon M Ulst..........61 M11

Dungarvan Kilken..........21 P6
Dungarvan/ *Dún Garbhán*
Watfd..........13 N10
Dungiven CC & G..........61 K2
Dungiven Priory CC & G..........61 K2
Dungloe/ *Dunglow/*
An Clochán Liath Donegl..........64 D11
Dunglow/ *Dungloe/*
An Clochán Liath Donegl..........64 D11
Dungourney Cork..........6 F6
Dunhill Watfd..........14 C8
Dún Ibhir/ *Dooniver*
Mayo..........40 F3
Dunkineely/ *Dún Cionnaola*
Donegl..........58 G8
Dún Laoghaire Dublin..........39 P9
Dunlavin/ *Dún Luáin*
Wicklw..........30 E5
Dunleer/ *Dún Léire* Louth..........47 L7
Dunloy CC & G..........67 Q10
Dunluce Castle CC & G..........67 N5
Dunmanway/
Dúnmaonmhuí Cork..........4 F6
Dunmore/ *Dún Mhór*
Kilken..........21 M3
Dunmore/ *Dún Mór*
Galway..........34 H2
Dunmore East/ *Dún Mór*
Watfd..........14 F8
Dunmurry Belfst..........62 H10
Dunnamaggan Kilken..........21 L8
Dunnamanagh/ *Donemana*
D & S..........60 E3
Dunquin/ *Dún Chaoin*
Kerry..........8 C5
Dunsany/ *Dún Samhna*
Meath..........38 H3
Dunseverick CC & G..........67 P5
Dunshaughlin/ *Dún*
Seachlainn Meath..........39 J4
Durrow Offaly..........37 K8
Durrow/ *Darú* Laois..........28 H10
Durrus/ *Dúrras* Cork..........3 P8
Dursey Island Cork..........2 E8
Dysart/ *An Díseart*
Roscom..........35 Q5
Dysart Cross Laois..........29 J9

E
Eadestown Kildre..........38 H11
Easky/ *Iascaigh* Sligo..........50 H6
EastSide Visitor Centre
Belfst..........63 K9
Edenderry/ *Éaden Doire*
Offaly..........38 B8
Edenfinfreagh/ *An tÉaden*
Anfach Donegl..........59 J5
Ederney F & O..........59 R11
Edgeworthstown/ *Meathas*
Troim Longfd..........45 J10
Effin Longfd..........18 F11
Effrinagh Leitrm..........44 D4
Eglinton D & S..........66 E9
Eglish M Ulst..........55 M2
Elphin/ *Ail Finn* Roscom..........43 Q7
Elton Limrck..........18 H9
Emly/ *Imleach* Tippry..........19 K9
Emo Laois..........29 K4
Emyvale/ *Scairbh na*
gCaorach Monhan..........55 K5
Enfield/ *An Bóthar Buí*
Meath..........38 E6
Enfield Services Kildre..........38 D6
Ennis/ *Inis* Clare..........25 M10
Enniscorthy/ *Inis Córthaidh*
Wexfd..........22 H8
Enniscrone/ *Inishcrone/Inis*
Crabhann Sligo..........50 F8
Enniskean/ *Inis Céin* Cork..........5 J6
Enniskerry/ *Áth na Sceire*
Wicklw..........31 M2
Enniskillen F & O..........53 Q5
Enniskillen Castle F & O..........53 Q5
Ennistymon/ *Ennistimon/*
Inis Díomáin Clare..........24 H8
Ennybegs Longfd..........44 G8
Erganagh D & S..........60 B6
Errew Mayo..........41 Q8
Errill Laois..........28 D10
Eskavaud Cork..........2 G7
Eskerbreague Offaly..........36 F8
Eyeries/ *Na hAoraí* Cork..........2 H6
Eyrecourt/ *Dún an Uchta*
Galway..........27 M2

F
Faha Galway..........35 K8
Fahamore Kerry..........9 J2
Fahan/ *Fathain* Donegl..........65 Q8
Fahy Mayo..........41 M7
Falcarragh/ *An Fál Carrach*
Donegl..........64 G7
Fanore/ *Fánóir* Clare..........24 H4
Farmleigh House Dublin..........39 L7
Farran Cork..........5 J10
Farran Cork..........5 K7
Farran Cork..........5 L3
Farran Cork..........11 M8
Farran Cork..........12 D10
Farranfore/ *An Fearann*
Fuar Kerry..........9 Q5
Farravaun Galway..........34 G7
Feakle/ *An Fhiacail* Clare..........26 E8
Fedamore/ *Feadamair*
Limrck..........18 F7
Feenagh Limrck..........18 C10
Feeny CC & G..........61 J2
Fenit/ *An Fhianait* Kerry..........9 L2
Fennagh Carlow..........22 D3
Fennor Watfd..........14 C8
Ferbane/ *An Féar Bán*
Offaly..........36 F10
Fermoy/ *Mainistir Fhear Maí*
Cork..........12 D9
Ferns/ *Fearna* Wexfd..........23 J6
Fertagh Bridge Kilken..........28 F11
Fethard/ *Fiodh Ard* Tippry..........20 F8
Fethard/ *Fiodh Ard*
Wexfd..........14 H7
Fews Watfd..........13 Q7
Fiddown/ *Fiodh Dúin*
Kilken..........14 B4
Fieries Kerry..........9 Q5
Finglas C Dubl..........39 M7
Fintona F & O..........60 E11
Fintown/ *Baile na Finne*
Donegl..........59 K3
Finvoy CC & G..........67 P10
Fionntrá/ *Ventry* Kerry..........8 D5
Fisherstown/ *Baile Fearainn*
Laois..........29 M4
Fivemiletown M Ulst..........54 E4
Florence Court F & O..........53 P7
Foher Cork..........2 G8
Foreglen CC & G..........61 J2
Forkhill NM & D..........56 C10
Fossa/ *An Fosadh* Kerry..........9 J2
Fota Wildlife Park Cork..........6 C7
Foulkesmill Wexfd..........15 K5
Fourmileburn A & N..........62 G6
Fourmilewater Watfd..........13 L6
Four Roads Roscom..........35 Q4
Foxford/ *Béal Easa* Mayo..........42 C4
Foxhole Cork..........7 J6
Foynes/ *Faing* Limrck..........17 M5
Freemount/ *Cillín an*
Chrónáin Cork..........11 J3
Frenchpark/ *Dún Gar*
Roscom..........43 M6
Freshford/ *Achadh Úr*
Kilken..........21 K3
Friarstown Dublin..........39 L10
Frosses/ *Na Frosa* Donegl..........58 H7
Fruit Hill Watfd..........13 N9
Furbo/ *Na Forbacha*
Galway..........33 Q10
Furkeal Cork..........3 P6
Furrow Cork..........12 E6

Garmna/ *Gorumna Island*
Galway..........33 J10
Garrafrauns Galway..........42 G11
Garrans Cross Laois..........29 L6
Garraun Cross Laois..........28 H10
Garrison F & O..........53 J3
Garristown Dublin..........39 L3
Garryduff Cork..........11 K5
Garrykennedy Tippry..........27 J9
Garrymore Offaly..........36 C10
Garrynageragh Watfd..........13 N10
Garryspillane Limrck..........19 J10
Garryvoe Cork..........6 G8
Garvagh CC & G..........67 L10
Garvagh Leitrm..........44 E4
Garvary F & O..........54 B4
Garvetagh D & S..........60 B7
Geashill/ *Géisill* Offaly..........37 N10
Geneva Cross Laois..........29 L10
George Best Belfast City
Airport Belfst..........63 K8
Giant's Causeway CC & G..........67 N5
Gibbstown/ *Baile Ghib*
Meath..........46 F10
Gilford AB & C..........56 D4
Gilroe Galway..........26 C7
Glandore/ *Cúan Dor* Cork..........4 F9
Glangevlin Cavan..........53 M8
Glanmire/ *Gleann Maghair*
Cork..........6 B7
Glanshanacuirp/ *Gleann*
Seandhoirp Kerry..........8 F4
Glansheskin Cork..........12 D8
Glanworth/ *Gleannúir* Cork..........12 C8
Glarryford E Antr..........68 B11
Glaslough/ *Glasloch*
Monhan..........55 L5
Glassamucky Dublin..........39 M10
Glassan/ *Glasán* Wmeath..........36 E5
Glastry A & ND..........63 Q11
Gleann Cholm Cille/
Glencolumbkille Donegl..........58 B7
Gleann na Muaidhe/
Glenamoy Mayo..........49 J7
Gleann Seandhoirp/
Glanshanacuirp Kerry..........8 F4
Glen Donegl..........65 L7
Glen Donegl..........65 N9
Glen Donegl..........66 C9
Glenamaddy/ *Gleann na*
Madadh Galway..........35 K2
Glenamoy/ *Gleann na*
Muaidhe Mayo..........49 J7
Glenarm E Antr..........68 G10
Glenavy L & C..........62 F9
Glenbeigh/ *Gleann Beithe*
Kerry..........9 K7
Glenbrien Wexfd..........23 J8
Glenbrook Cork..........6 C8
Glencar Kerry..........9 L9
Glencolumbkille/
Cholm Cille Donegl..........58 B7
Glencoria Wicklw..........31 L6
Glencullen/ *Gleann Cuilinn*
Dublin..........39 N10
Glendalough/ *Gleann Dá*
Loch Wicklw..........31 K6
Glendalough Monastic
Site Wicklw..........31 K6
Glenealy/ *Gleann*
Fhaidhle Wicklw..........31 M7
Gleneely Donegl..........66 E5
Glengarriff/ *An Gleann*
Garbh Cork..........3 P5
Glengormley A & N..........63 J7
Glenisland Mayo..........41 N5
Glenmalure Wicklw..........31 K7
Glenoe E Antr..........63 K4
Glenroe Limrck..........12 B5
Glenties/ *Na Gleannta*
Donegl..........58 H5
Glenveagh Castle Donegl..........65 J9
Glenveagh National
Park Donegl..........65 J10
Glenville/ *Gleann an*
Phréacháin Cork..........6 B8
Glin/ *An Gleann* Limrck..........17 K6
Glounthaune Cork..........6 C7
Glynn Carlow..........22 C8
Glynn E Antr..........63 L4
Glynn Wexfd..........15 M9
Goatanbridge Tippry..........13 J6
Goatstown Dublin..........39 N9
Gob an Choire/ *Achill Sound*
Mayo..........40 F5
Goggins Hill Cork..........5 P4

Golden/ *An Gabhailín*
Tippry.................................19 Q8
Goleen/ *An Góilín* Cork............ 3 M11
Goresbridge/ *An Droichead*
Nua Kilken...........................22 B5
Gorey/ *Guaire* Wexfd...........23 M4
Gorey Services Wexfd...........23 N2
Gormanston/ *Baile Mhic*
Gormáin Meath 47 N11
Gort/ *Gort Inse Guaire*
Galway...............................26 C5
Gortaghig Cork...................... 2 G7
Gortahork/ *Gort an Choirce*
Donegl...............................64 G7
Gort an Choirce/ *Gortahork*
Donegl...............................64 G7
Gortbreagoge Kerry........... 9 J5
Gorteen Sligo.......................43 L3
Gortin F & O.........................60 F6
Gortletteragh Leitrm...........44 F6
Gortlicka Kerry..................... 3 N3
Gortnaclohy Cork................ 4 D10
Gortnahoe/ *Gort na hUamha*
Tippry.................................20 G4
Gortnahultra Galway...........35 K7
Gortnakilla Kerry.................10 C9
Gortnaskehy Cork................12 F7
Gortroe Cork......................... 3 Q5
Gortroe Kerry....................... 9 Q7
Gorumna Island/ *Garmna*
Galway...............................33 J10
Gougane Barra/ *Guagán*
Barra Cork.......................... 4 C3
Gour Cork.............................. 2 H8
Gowna Cavan......................45 K6
Gowran/ *Gabhrán* Kilken.....21 P5
Gracehill E Antr...................62 D3
Graig Cork............................11 Q3
Graigue Cross Laois.............29 K8
Graiguenamanagh/ *Gráig na*
Manach Kilken 22 C7
Granard/ *Gránard* Longfd....45 K8
Grange Kilken......................21 L5
Grange Louth.......................47 N3
Grange Tippry......................20 H4
Grange/ *An Ghráinseach*
Sligo.................................52 D4
Grangebellew Louth............47 L7
Grange Con Wicklw.............30 D7
Grangeford Bridge Kildre....30 C8
Granville M Ulst...................61 M11
Greencastle Donegl.............66 H5
Greencastle F & O...............60 H7
Greenisland E Antr..............63 K6
Greenore/ *An Grianfort*
Louth.................................47 P2
Gregory's Cross Roads
Laois.................................29 M9
Grenagh Cork......................11 N9
Greyabbey A & ND...............63 P10
Greysteel CC & G.................66 F9
Greystones/ *Na Clocha Liatha*
Wicklw...............................31 N3
Groomsport A & ND.............63 N7
Guagán Barra/ *Gougane*
Barra Cork.......................... 4 C3
Guinness Storehouse
C Dubl...............................39 M8
Gulladuff M Ulst...................61 P4
Gun Point Cork..................... 3 N11
Gurteen Galway....................35 K7
Gurteen Leitrm.....................52 F5
Gurteens Mayo.....................50 E10
Gusserane Wexfd.................14 H5
Gweedore/ *Gaoth Dobhair*
Donegl...............................64 F9
Gweesalia/ *Gaoth Sáile*
Mayo.................................48 G9
Gyles Quay Louth.................47 N3

H

Hacketstown/ *Baile Haicéid*
Carlow...............................30 G9
Halfway Cork......................... 5 P4
Hamiltons Bawn AB & C.......55 Q5
Hammondstown Louth..........47 K7
Harestown Louth..................47 L8
Harristown Kildre..................29 N4
Hawksford Roscom...............43 J5
Headford/ *Áth Cinn*
Galway...............................34 C5
Helen's Bay A & ND..............63 M7
Hell Kettle Bridge Wicklw....30 F6

Hennebry's Cross Kilken......21 L3
Herbertstown/ *Baile*
Hiobaird Limrck................18 H7
Hillhall L & C.........................62 H11
Hill of Tara Meath................38 H3
Hill of The O'Neill Visitor
Centre M Ulst.....................61 M11
Hillsborough L & C...............56 G2
Hilltown Donegl....................58 G7
Hilltown NM & D...................56 G8
Hilltown Wexfd.....................15 K6
Hollyford Tippry....................19 N5
Hollyfort Wexfd....................23 L3
Hollymount Mayo.................42 C11
Hollywood/ *Cillín Chaoimhín*
Wicklw...............................30 F4
Holycross Limrck..................18 G8
Holycross Tippry...................20 C5
Holycross Abbey Tippry.......20 C5
Holywood A & ND.................63 L8
Horse and Jockey Tippry.....20 E5
Horseleap Wmeath...............37 J7
Hospital/ *An tOspidéal*
Limrck...............................19 J8
Howth/ *Binn Éadair* Dublin..39 Q7
Hugginstown Kilken.............21 M9
Huntsman Cross Carlow......22 D2

I

Inagh/ *Eidhneach* Clare........25 K9
Inch Kerry.............................. 9 J5
Inch/ *An Inis* Wexfd..............23 M2
Inches Cork........................... 3 J7
Inchicloon Kerry.................... 3 N3
Inchigeelagh/ *Inse*
Geimhleach Cork.............. 4 F3
Inchinattin Cross Roads
Cork.................................. 4 G8
Inchintaggart Cork............... 3 P5
Inchinteskin Cork.................. 2 H7
Indreabhán/ *Inverin*
Galway...............................33 M10
Inis Bó Finne/ *Inishbofin*
Galway...............................40 B11
Inis Crabhann/ *Inishcrone/*
Enniscrone Sligo..............50 F8
Inishbofin/ *Inis Bó Finne*
Galway...............................40 B11
Inishcrone/ *Enniscrone/Inis*
Crabhann Sligo................50 F8
Inisheer/ *Inis Oírr* Galway....24 E5
Inishmaan/ *Inis Meáin*
Galway...............................24 D5
Inishmore/ *Inis Mór*
Galway...............................24 B4
Inishowen Donegl.................66 C5
Inishturk/ *Inis Toirc* Mayo....40 D10
Inis Meáin/ *Inishmaan*
Galway...............................24 D5
Inis Mór/ *Inishmore*
Galway...............................24 B4
Inis Oírr/ *Inisheer* Galway....24 E5
Inistioge/ *Inis Tíog* Kilken....21 P8
Inis Toirc/ *Inishturk* Mayo....40 D10
Innishannon/ *Inis Eonáin*
Cork.................................. 5 M5
Inniskeen/ *Inis Caoin*
Monahan............................46 H3
Innisrush M Ulst...................61 Q3
Inver/ *Inbhear* Donegl..........58 H8
Inverin/ *Indreabhán*
Galway...............................33 M10
Ireland West Airport
Knock Mayo........................42 G5
Irish Linen Centre &
Lisburn Museum L & C.....62 H11
Irish Museum of Modern
Art C Dubl...........................39 M8
Irish National Stud &
Japanese Gardens
Kildre.................................29 P3
Irishtown Mayo.....................42 F11
Irvinestown F & O.................53 Q2
Iscaheen Donegl...................66 D8
Islandmagee E Antr..............63 M4
Iveragh Peninsula/ *Uíbh*
Ráthach Kerry..................... 8 F8

J

Jameson Experience
Cork.................................. 6 E7
Jenkinstown Kilken..............21 L2

Jerpoint Abbey Kilken..........21 N7
Jerrettspass NM & D.............56 D7
John F Kennedy
Arboretum Wexfd.............14 G5
Johnstown Cork.................... 4 G4
Johnstown Meath.................46 G11
Johnstown Wicklw................30 G4
Johnstown/ *Baile Eoin*
Kildre.................................38 H10
Johnstown/ *Baile Sheáin*
Kilken................................20 G2
Johnstown Bridge Kildre.....38 E7
Johns Well Kilken.................21 N3
Jonesborough NM & D..........56 D10
Jordanstown A & N...............63 K7
Julianstown Meath...............47 M11
Junction 14 Mayfield
Services Kildre..................29 N3

K

Kanturk/ *Ceann Toirc* Cork...11 J5
Katesbridge AB & C..............56 G5
Keadue/ *Céideadh* Roscom..44 B2
Keady AB & C.........................55 N7
Kealkill Cork......................... 4 B5
Keane's Crossroads Cork....12 E7
Keating's Cross Laois...........29 L8
Keel/ *An Caol* Mayo.............40 D4
Keelbanada Roscom.............43 L5
Keeloges Mayo.....................42 B6
Kells E Antr...........................62 E4
Kells Kerry............................ 8 H8
Kells/ *Ceanannas* Kilken......21 L7
Kells/ *Ceanannas* Meath.....46 D9
Kelly's Cross Laois...............28 H9
Kellyville Laois.....................29 M7
Kenagh/ *Caonach* Longfd....36 F2
Kenmare/ *Neidín* Kerry........ 3 P2
Kentstown Meath.................47 J11
Kerry Airport Kerry.............. 9 R5
Kerrykeel/ *An Cheathrú*
Chaol Donegl.....................65 N7
Kerry Pike Cork.....................11 P11
Kesh F & O.............................59 Q11
Keshcarrigan Leitrm.............44 D3
Kielduff Kerry........................ 9 Q2
Kilanerin Wexfd.....................23 M2
Kilbaha/ *Cill Bheathach*
Clare................................16 B6
Kilbeggan/ *Cill*
Bheagáin Wmeath...........37 K7
Kilbehenny Limrck................12 E5
Kilberry Kildre.......................29 N6
Kilberry Meath......................46 G10
Kilbraghan/ *Cill Bhearcháin*
Kilken................................21 J6
Kilbride Meath......................39 L5
Kilbrien Watfd.......................13 M8
Kilbrin/ *Cill Bhrain* Cork......11 K4
Kilbrittain/ *Cill Briotáin*
Cork.................................. 5 M7
Kilcar/ *Cill Charthaigh*
Donegl...............................58 D8
Kilcatherine Cork.................. 2 H6
Kilchreest/ *Cill Chríost*
Galway...............................26 E3
Kilclief NM & D......................57 P4
Kilclogh Cork........................12 D8
Kilclone/ *Coill Chluana*
Meath................................38 H6
Kilcloon/ *Chill Chluana*
Meath................................38 H6
Kilcock/ *Cill Choca* Meath....38 G7
Kilcogy Cavan.......................45 L7
Kilcolgan/ *Cill Cholgáin*
Galway...............................34 F11
Kilcolman Limrck..................17 N7
Kilconly Galway.....................34 E3
Kilconnell Galway.................35 M8
Kilcoo NM & D.......................56 H7
Kilcoole/ *Cill Chomhghaill*
Wicklw...............................31 N4
Kilcormac/ *Cill Chormaic*
Offaly................................28 C3
Kilcrohane Cork..................... 3 M9
Kilcullen/ *Cill Chuillinn*
Kildre.................................30 D4
Kilcullen Services Kildre.......30 D4
Kilcummin Kerry.................... 8 H3
Kilcummin Kerry...................10 A6
Kilcurly Louth.......................47 K3
Kildalkey Meath....................38 D3
Kildangan Kildre...................29 N4
Kildare/ *Cill Dara* Kildre.......29 P3

Kildavin Carlow.....................22 F3
Kildoney Donegl....................60 A4
Kildoon Kildre.......................29 P4
Kildorrery/ *Cill Dairbhre*
Cork.................................12 B6
Kildrum Cork.........................12 E6
Kildrum Donegl.....................66 B11
Kilfenora/ *Cill Fhionnúrach*
Clare.................................25 J7
Kilfinane/ *Cill Fhíonáin*
Limrck...............................18 H11
Kilflynn Kerry.......................16 E11
Kilgarvan/ *Cill Garbháin*
Kerry.................................10 B11
Kilgobnet Watfd....................13 M9
Kilkea/ *Cill Cathaigh* Kildre..29 P8
Kilkee/ *Cill Chaoi* Clare.......16 E4
Kilkeel NM & D......................57 J11
Kilkelly/ *Cill Cheallaigh*
Mayo.................................42 F6
Kilkenny/ *Cill Chainnigh*
Kilken................................21 M4
Kilkenny Castle Kilken.........21 M4
Kilkieran/ *Cill Chiaráin*
Galway...............................32 H8
Kilkishen/ *Cill Chisín* Clare..26 C11
Kill Cavan.............................45 Q3
Kill Watfd..............................14 B8
Kill/ *An Chill* Kildre...............38 H10
Killadysert Clare...................17 N4
Killaha East Kerry................. 3 P3
Killala/ *Cill Ala* Mayo...........50 E7
Killaloe Clare........................26 H11
Killaloo D & S.......................60 G2
Killan Galway........................35 M4
Killanena Clare.....................26 D7
Killann/ *Cill Anna* Wexfd.....22 F7
Killaphort Offaly...................36 C10
Killarga/ *Cill Fhearga*
Leitrm...............................52 H7
Killarney/ *Cill Airne* Kerry.... 9 R7
Killarney National Park
Kerry................................. 9 R10
Killashandra/ *Cill na*
Seanrátha Cavan.............45 K3
Killashee Longfd...................44 E10
Killasmeestia Laois..............28 D9
Killavullen/ *Cill an Mhuilinn*
Cork.................................11 P6
Killawalla Mayo.....................41 N9
Killea D & S...........................63 B11
Killea Leitrm.........................53 J3
Killea Tippry.........................27 Q11
Killea Watfd..........................14 F8
Killead A & N.........................62 F7
Killeagh/ *Cill Ia* Cork........... 6 H6
Killedmond Carlow................22 D5
Killeen Galway......................26 C7
Killeen Laois.........................29 N9
Killeen Mayo.........................40 G9
Killeevan Monahan...............54 H8
Killeigh/ *Cill Aichidh* Offaly...37 L11
Killen D & S...........................60 A8
Killenard Laois.....................29 L4
Killenaule/ *Cill Náile*
Tippry.................................20 E6
Killeshin Laois......................29 N10
Killeter D & S.........................59 R7
Killimer Clare........................17 J5
Killimor/ *Cill Íomair*
Galway...............................27 K3
Killina Offaly.........................37 J10
Killinaboy/ *Cill Iníne Baoith*
Clare.................................25 L7
Killinchy A & ND....................63 N11
Killiney/ *Cill Iníon Léinín*
Dublin...............................39 Q9
Killinick Wexfd......................15 K9
Killinkere Cavan....................46 B6
Killorglin/ *Cill Orglan*
Kerry................................. 9 M6
Killoscully Tippry...................19 K2
Killough Cork........................ 2 E4
Killough NM & D....................57 N6
Killowen NM & D....................56 F10
Killucan/ *Cill Liúcainne*
Wmeath.............................37 Q4
Killult/ *Cill Ulta* Donegl........64 F3
Killurin Offaly........................37 K11
Killurin Wexfd.......................15 M3
Killybegs/ *Na Cealla Beaga*
Donegl...............................58 F8
Killydoon Cavan....................45 L6
Killyfaddy AB & C..................55 P6
Killygordon/ *Cúil na*
gCuirridín Donegl..............59 R5

Killylea AB & C **55** M4
Killyleagh NM & D **57** N3
Killyman M Ulst **61** N11
Killyon Offaly **28** B4
Killyrammer CC & G **67** P8
Kilmacanogue/ *Cill*
  Mocheanóg Wicklw **31** M3
Kilmacow/ *Cill Mhic Bhúith*
  Kilken **14** D5
Kilmacrenan/ *Cill Mhic*
  Réanáin Donegl **65** L9
Kilmacthomas/ *Coill Mhic*
  Thomáisín Watfd **13** Q7
Kilmaganny/ *Cill Mogeanna*
  Kilken **21** L9
Kilmaine Mayo **34** C3
Kilmainham Gaol C Dubl **39** M8
Kilmainham Wood Meath **46** E7
Kilmaley Clare **25** K10
Kilmallock/ *Cill*
  Mocheallóg Limrck **18** G10
Kilmanagh/ *Cill Mhanach*
  Kilken **21** J5
Kilmead/ *Cill Míde* Kildre **29** P6
Kilmeadan Watfd **14** C7
Kilmeage/ *Cill Maodhóg*
  Kildre **38** E10
Kilmeedy/ *Cill Míde*
  Limrck **18** B10
Kilmessan Meath **38** G3
Kilmichael Cork **4** G3
Kilmihil/ *Cill Mhichíl* Clare....**17** K3
Kilmore AB & C **55** Q3
Kilmore Mayo **42** C4
Kilmore NM & D **57** L3
Kilmore/ *An Chill Mhór*
  Wexfd............................**15** M7
Kilmore Quay/ *Cé na Cille*
  Móire Wexfd...................**15** M8
Kilmovee Mayo **42** H6
Kilmoyly Kerry **16** C10
Kilmuckridge/ *Cill*
  Mhucraise Wexfd...........**23** M7
Kilmurry Clare **24** F11
Kilmurry Limrck **5** J3
Kilmurry Limrck **18** H10
Kilmurry Wicklw **30** F8
Kilmurry/ *Cill Mhuire* Clare ..**18** D2
Kilmyshall Wexfd.................**22** G5
Kilnafrehan Watfd **13** N9
Kilnaleck/ *Cill na Leice*
  Cavan **45** M6
Kilnamona Clare **25** L9
Kilpedder/ *Cill Pheadair*
  Wicklw **31** N4
Kilquade/ *Cill Chomhaid*
  Wicklw **31** N4
Kilraghts CC & G **67** Q8
Kilrane Wexfd.....................**15** Q6
Kilrea CC & G **67** N11
Kilreekill/ *Cill Rícill*
  Galway **35** L10
Kilronan/ *Cill Rónáin*
  Galway **24** C4
Kilross Tippry **19** L9
Kilruane Tippry **27** M9
Kilrush/ *Cill Rois* Clare **16** G4
Kilsaran Louth **47** L6
Kilshane Cross Dublin..........**39** M6
Kilshannig Kerry **9** J2
Kilsheelan Tippry **13** N4
Kilskeery F & O **54** B3
Kilskyre Meath **46** C10
Kiltannon Clare **26** C9
Kiltealy/ *Cill Téile* Wexfd......**22** F6
Kilteel Kildre **39** J10
Kiltely/ *Cill Tíle* Limrck.........**19** J7
Kiltegan Wicklw **30** F9
Kiltegan Bridge Wicklw........**30** F9
Kilternan Dublin **39** P10
Kiltimagh/ *Coillte Mach*
  Mayo **42** D7
Kiltormer/ *Cill Tormóir*
  Galway **35** P10
Kiltyclogher/ *Coillte Clochair*
  Leitrm **53** K4
Kilwaughter E Antr **63** K3
Kilworth/ *Cill Uird* Cork........**12** D8
Kinallen AB & C **56** H4
Kinawley F & O **53** Q7
Kincasslagh/ *Cionn Caslach*
  Donegl **64** C10
King John's Castle
  Limrck **18** F4
Kingscourt/ *Dún an Rí*
  Cavan **46** E3

Kinlough/ *Cionn Locha*
  Leitrm **52** G2
Kinnegad/ *Cionn Átha*
  Gad Wmeath **37** Q5
Kinnitty/ *Cionn Eitigh*
  Offaly **28** C4
Kinsale/ *Cionn tSáile* Cork ... **5** P6
Kinvarra/ *Cinn Mhara*
  Galway **25** N3
Kircubbin A & ND **63** P11
Kirkistown A & ND **57** Q2
Kiskeam Cork **10** F5
Knappagh/ *An Chnapach*
  Mayo **41** L8
Knightstown Kerry **8** E10
Knock Clare **17** J5
Knock Tippry **28** D8
Knock/ *Cnoc Mhuire* Mayo ...**42** E8
Knockaderry Limrck **17** P8
Knockadireen Kerry **16** H10
Knockainey/ *Cnoc Áine*
  Limrck **18** H8
Knockalougha Kerry **16** H10
Knockananna Wicklw **30** H9
Knockanean Clare **25** N10
Knockaroe Laois **28** E8
Knockawaddra West
  Kerry **9** P2
Knockbrack Galway..............**34** H8
Knockbracken L & C **63** K10
Knockbridge/ *Droichead an*
  Chnoic Louth..................**47** J4
Knockcarren Limrck **19** K9
Knockcloghrim M Ulst **61** P4
Knockcroghery/ *Cnoc an*
  Chrochaire Roscom **36** B3
Knockduff Kerry **3** P4
Knockgour Cork **2** H8
Knocklong Limrck **19** J9
Knockmahon Watfd.............**14** A9
Knockmore Mayo.................**42** B3
Knocknacally Cork **7** J6
Knocknacarry CC & G **68** E7
Knocknagashel Kerry **17** J11
Knocknagree Cork **10** E6
Knocknalina/ *Cnocán na*
  Líne Mayo **48** G6
Knockraha Cork **6** C6
Knockroe Cork **2** G8
Knocktopher/ *Cnoc an*
  Tóchair Kilken **21** M8
Kylemore Galway **27** J4
Kylemore Abbey &
  Gardens Galway **32** F3

Labasheeda Clare **17** L5
Lack F & O **60** B10
Lackagh Galway...................**34** F7
Lacken Wicklw.....................**30** H3
Ladysbridge Cork **6** G7
Lagavooren Meath...............**47** L10
Laghy/ *An Lathaigh*
  Donegl **59** K9
Laharan Kerry **9** P2
Lahardane Mayo **41** P3
Lahinch/ *Leacht Uí*
  Chonchubhair Clare **24** G8
Lanesborough/ *Béal Átha*
  Liag Longfd **44** D11
Laragh Kildre **38** G7
Laragh Monhan **46** E2
Laragh/ *An Láithreach*
  Wicklw **31** K6
Laragh Cavan **45** P3
Larchfield Cross Laois..........**29** J8
Largy Donegl **58** E8
Larkin's Cross Laois **29** K9
Larne E Antr **63** L3
Larry Cross Laois **28** F8
Lattin Tippry **19** L8
Lauragh/ *An Láithreach*
  Kerry **3** L5
Laurelvale AB & C **56** C4
Laurencetown/ *An Baile Mór*
  Galway **35** Q10
Lavey/ *Leamhaí* Cavan **45** P4
Lawrencetown AB & C **56** D4
Laytown/ *An Inse* Meath.....**47** N10
Leabeg Offaly **36** G9
Leaby Cross Louth **47** J8
Leap/ *An Léim* Cork............. **4** F9
Lecanvey/ *Leac an Anfa*
  Mayo **41** J8

Leckemy Donegl **66** F5
Leenaun/ *Lionán* Galway **33** J2
Legan Longfd **36** H2
Leggah Longfd **44** H6
Leighlinbridge/ *Leithghlinn*
  an Droichid Carlow **22** B2
Leitir Mhic an Bhaird/
  Lettermacaward Donegl ...**58** G3
Leitir Móir/ *Lettermore*
  Galway **33** J9
Leitreach Ard/ *Letterard*
  Galway **32** G7
Leitrim/ *Liatroim* Leitrm......**44** C4
Leixlip Kildre.......................**39** K7
Lemanaghan Offaly **36** G9
Lemybrien Watfd.................**13** P8
Lenadery AB & C **56** E4
Letterard/ *Leitreach Ard*
  Galway **32** G7
Letterbreen F & O **53** P5
Letterfrack/ *Leitir Fraic*
  Galway **32** F3
Letterkenny/ *Leitir*
  Ceanainn Donegl **65** M11
Letterkern F & O **59** Q10
Lettermacaward/ *Leitir Mhic*
  an Bhaird Donegl............**58** G3
Lettermore/ *Leitir Móir*
  Galway **33** J9
Lickbarrahane Cork **2** H8
Lifford/ *Leifear* Donegl........**60** C4
Limavady CC & G **66** H9
Limerick/ *Luimneach*
  Limrck **18** F4
Limerick City Gallery of
  Art Limrck **18** F4
Limerick Junction Tippry **19** M8
Lios Póil/ *Lispole* Kerry......... **8** G5
Lisacul Roscom **43** J6
Lisbane A & ND **63** M11
Lisbellaw F & O **54** C5
Lisburn L & C **62** H11
Lisburn Services L & C **62** H10
Liscannor/ *Lios Ceannúir*
  Clare **24** G8
Liscarney/ *Lios Cearnaigh*
  Mayo **41** L9
Liscarroll/ *Lios Cearúill*
  Cork **11** L3
Lisdoonvarna/ *Lios Dúin*
  Bhearna Clare **24** H6
Lisgoold Cork **6** E5
Liscmcaffrey Wmeath..........**45** L10
Lismonaghan Donegl **59** Q2
Lismore Kerry **9** P2
Lismore/ *Lios Mór* Watfd.....**12** H9
Lismoyny Wmeath **37** J8
Lismulleyduff Donegl **59** Q6
Lisnagunnion Monhan **46** F3
Lisnamoyle Monhan **46** G3
Lisnarrick F & O **53** P2
Lisnaskea F & O **54** D7
Lispole/ *Lios Póil* Kerry **8** G5
Lisronagh Tippry **20** F10
Lisryan Longfd **45** K9
Lisselton Cross Kerry **16** F8
Lissycasey Clare **17** M2
Listack Donegl **59** P2
Listowel/ *Lios Tuathail*
  Kerry **16** G9
Lisvarrinane Tippry **19** L10
Little Island Cork **6** C7
Littleton/ *An Baile Beag*
  Tippry **20** E5
Lixnaw/ *Leic Snámha* Kerry ...**16** E10
Lochan Iúir/ *Loghanure*
  Donegl **64** E10
Loch Coirib/ *Lough Corrib*
  Galway **33** P5
Loch Measca/ *Lough Mask*
  Mayo **33** P2
Lombardstown Cork **11** L6
Londonderry/ *Derry*
  D & S **66** C10
Longford Offaly **28** C5
Longford/ *An Longfort*
  Longfd **44** F9
Longford Cross Laois **28** E6
Longwood Meath **38** D5
Lordship Louth....................**47** M3
Lorrha/ *Lothra* Tippry.........**27** M5
Lough Clare **24** G8
Loughananna Limrck **12** E5
Loughanure/ *Lochan Iúir*
  Donegl **64** E10
Loughbrickland AB & C.........**56** E5

Lough Corrib/ *Loch Coirib*
  Galway **33** P5
Loughcrew Cairns Meath.....**45** Q9
Lough Derg Tippry **26** H9
Loughduff Cavan **45** L6
Lough Foyle CC & G..............**66** F8
Loughgall AB & C **55** Q3
Loughglinn/ *Loch Glinne*
  Roscom **43** K7
Loughguile CC & G **68** B8
Lough Hill Clare **26** H7
Loughinisland NM & D..........**57** L4
Loughlahan Tippry **20** E3
Lough Mask/ *Loch Measca*
  Mayo **33** P2
Loughmore Tippry **20** D2
Loughnanemore Cork **2** F8
Loughnavalley Wmeath........**37** K5
Lough Neagh A & N **62** U8
Loughrea/ *Baile Locha Riach*
  Galway **26** F2
Lough Ree Roscom **36** D4
Loughshinny/ *Loch Sionnach*
  Dublin **39** Q3
Louisburgh/ *Cluain Cearbán*
  Mayo **40** H8
Louis Mulcahy Pottery
  Kerry **8** C5
Louth/ *Lú* Louth **47** J4
Lower Ballinderry L & C.........**62** E10
Lower Lough Erne F & O........**53** N2
Lucan Dublin **39** K7
Lumville Cross Kildre............**30** C3
Lurgan AB & C **56** D2
Lurgankiel Louth **47** K2
Lusk/ *Lusca* Dublin.............**39** P4
Lusk Services Dublin............**39** N3
Lyracrumpane Kerry **16** G11
Lyre Cork **5** J7
Lyre Cork **6** G4
Lyre Cork **11** K7
Lyre Kerry **10** C3

M

Maam Cross/ *An Teach Dóite*
  Galway **33** L5
Machaire Rabhartaigh/
  Magheraroarty Donegl **64** F7
Macosquin CC & G **67** L8
Macroney Cork **12** E8
Macroom/ *Maigh Chromtha*
  Cork **10** H11
Maghaberry L & C.................**62** F11
Maghera Cavan **46** B8
Maghera M Ulst **61** P3
Maghera NM & D **57** K7
Magherafelt M Ulst **61** P3
Magheralin AB & C **56** E2
Magherally AB & C **56** F4
Magheramason D & S **66** B11
Magheramorne E Antr.........**63** L4
Magheraroarty/ *Machaire*
  Rabhartaigh Donegl **64** F7
Magheraveely/ *Machaire*
  Mhílic F & O **54** F8
Maghery AB & C **61** Q11
Maghery/ *Mhachaire*
  Donegl **58** C2
Maguiresbridge F & O...........**54** C6
Mahoonagh Limrck **17** P9
Maigh Cuilinn/
  Moycullen Galway **34** B8
Maíghros/ *Moyrus* Galway...**32** G8
Malahide/ *Mullach Íde*
  Dublin **39** P5
Malahide Castle & Gardens
  Dublin **39** P5
Málainn Bhig/ *Malin Beg*
  Donegl **58** A7
Málainn Mhóir/ *Malin More*
  Donegl **58** A7
Malin/ *Málainn* Donegl........**66** D3
Malin Beg/ *Málainn Bhig*
  Donegl **58** A7
Malin Head Donegl **66** B2
Malin More/ *Málainn Mhóir*
  Donegl **58** B7
Mallow/ *Mala* Cork.............**11** N6
Mallusk A & N **62** H10
Manorcunningham/
  Mainéar Uí Chuinneagáin
  Donegl **65** N11
Manorhamilton/ *Cluainín*
  Leitrm **52** H3

Manor Stone Services
Laois 28 G10
Mansfieldstown Louth......47 K5
Manulla Mayo 42 B7
Marble Arch Caves F & O....53 N7
Markethill AB & C................56 B6
Marlfield Tippry 13 L4
Marshalstown Wexfd........22 H6
Martinstown E Antr 68 C11
Maulatrahane Cross Roads
Cork 4 E9
Mayglass Wexfd................15 N6
Maynooth/ Maigh Nuad
Kildre 38 M7
Mayo Abbey Mayo 42 C9
Mayobridge NM & D.........56 F8
Mazetown L & C 62 G11
McCormack's Cross
Laois 29 K8
McNead's Bridge Wmeath....37 P5
Meanus Limrck..................18 F4
Meelick Clare.....................18 F3
Meenacarn/ Min an Chairn
Donegl.................................58 G3
Meenanare Kerry..............16 H10
Meenscovane Kerry.........17 J11
Meigh NM & D....................56 D9
Melview Longfd.................44 F9
Menlough/ Mionlach
Galway 35 K6
Mhachaire/ Maghery
Donegl.................................58 F2
Middletown AB & C...........55 M6
Midleton/ Mainister na Corann
Cork 6 E7
Milestone Tippry 19 N4
Milford AB & C 55 P5
Milford/ Áth an Mhuilinn
Cork 18 C11
Milford/ Baile na
nGallóglach Donegl.............65 M8
Millbrook E Antr 63 K3
Millbrook Meath................45 P9
Milleen Bridge Cork 4 E9
Millisle A & ND...................63 P8
Millstreet Cork...................12 E7
Millstreet Watfd.................13 L8
Millstreet/ Sráid an Mhuilinn
Cork 10 G7
Milltown AB & C................55 N3
Milltown Cavan.................54 C11
Milltown CC & G 67 K7
Milltown Dublin 39 K8
Milltown Galway................34 F2
Milltown Kildre 38 E11
Milltown L & C 62 H10
Milltown/ Baile an Mhuilinn
Kerry 8 E5
Milltown/ Baile an Mhuilinn
Kerry 9 N5
Milltown Malbay/ Sráid na
Cathrach Clare....................24 G10
Milltownpass Wmeath 37 P6
Mín an Chairn/ Meenacarn
Donegl.................................58 G3
Minane Bridge/ Droichead an
Mhionnáin Cork 6 B10
Mitchelstown/ Baile
Mhistéala Cork 12 D6
Mitchelstown Cave
Tippry 12 F5
Moate/ An Móta Wmeath 36 G2
Modelligo Watfd.................13 L9
Model Village Cork............11 L10
Mogeely Cork 6 G6
Mohill/ Maothail Leitrm......44 E5
Moira L & C 62 E11
Monagear/ Móin na gCaor
Wexfd..................................23 J7
Monaghan/ Muineachán
Monhan 55 N7
Monamolin Wexfd..............23 L6
Monard Tippry 19 L8
Monaseed Wexfd...............23 K3
Monaster Limrck................18 E7
Monasteraden Sligo..........43 L5
Monasterevin/ Mainistir
Eimhín Kildre 29 M3
Monavea Cross Laois........29 M10
Monea F & O........................53 P3
Moneygall/ Muine Gall
Offaly 27 P9
Moneygall Services
Tippry 27 P9
Moneyglass A & N..............62 C5
Moneymore M Ulst............61 P7

Moneyneany M Ulst...........61 L4
Moneyreagh L & C 63 L10
Moneyslane AB & C 56 G6
Moneystown Wicklw.........31 M6
Monivea/ Muine Mheá
Galway 34 H7
Monkstown/ Baile an
Mhanaigh Cork 6 C8
Monmore Clare 16 G4
Montpelier Limrck 18 H2
Mooncoin/ Móin Choinn
Kilken 14 C5
Mooney's Cross Laois........29 M9
Moorepark Services
Cork 12 D8
Moore's Cross Laois.........29 M10
Moorfields E Antr...............62 F4
Mornington Meath 47 M9
Morriscastle Wexfd...........23 M7
Moss-Side CC & G 67 Q6
Mountain Barrack/
Red Hill Cork 12 E7
Mountbellew/ An Creagán
Galway 35 L5
Mountbolus Offaly.............28 D2
Mountcharles/ Moin Séarlas
Donegl.................................59 J8
Mountcollins Limrck 10 E2
Mountfield F & O 60 G8
Mountjoy F & O...................60 E8
Mountjoy M Ulst................61 Q10
Mountmellick/ Móinteach
Mílic Laois..........................29 J4
Mount Nugent Cavan........45 N7
Mountrath/ Maighean Rátha
Laois 28 G2
Mount Rivers Watfd 13 K9
Mountshannon/ Baile Uí
Bheoláin Clare 26 H8
Mount Stewart House &
Gardens A & ND 63 P10
Mount Talbot Roscom........35 P4
Mount Uniacke Cork 6 G5
Mount Usher Gardens
Wicklw 31 N6
Mourne Mountains
NM & D................................56 H9
Moville/ Bun an Phobail
Donegl.................................66 G6
Moy Galway........................25 N4
Moy M Ulst 55 N2
Moycullen/ Maigh Cuilinn
Galway 38 B8
Moydow Longfd.................44 F11
Moygashel M Ulst..............61 N11
Moyglare Meath 38 H7
Moyglass Galway...............26 G5
Moylough Galway..............35 K5
Moylough Sligo.................42 H3
Moyna Mayo.......................41 L7
Moynalty Meath 46 D8
Moyne Tippry 20 E3
Moyrhee Clare 25 N7
Moyrus/ Maighros Galway 32 J8
Moys Clare 26 H11
Moyvally Kildre 38 D6
Moyvane/ Maigh Mheáin
Kerry 17 J8
Moyvore Wmeath...............37 J4
Muckalee Kilken................21 N2
Mucklagh Offaly................37 K10
Mucklagh Bridge Wicklw....31 J8
Muckross House Kerry 9 R8
Muff/ Magh Donegl............66 D9
Mulhuddart Services
Dublin..................................39 L6
Mullagh Galway................35 M11
Mullagh Meath..................38 H5
Mullagh/ An Mullach
Cavan..................................46 C7
Mullagh/ Mullach Clare.......24 F11
Mullaghbane NM & D.........56 B10
Mullaghmore/ An Mullach
Mór Sligo 52 E2
Mullan's Corner AB & C.....56 F7
Mullinacuft Wicklw...........30 G11
Mullinahone/ Muileann na
hUaman Tippry 20 H7
Mullinalaghta Longfd.........45 K7
Mullinavat/ Muileann an
Bhata Kilken 14 D4
Mullingar/ An Muileann
gCearr Wmeath...................37 M4
Mullyleggan Bridge
AB & C.................................55 N3
Mulranny Mayo..................40 H5

Multyfarnham/ Muilte
Farannáin Wmeath 37 M2
Mungret/ Mungairit Limrck....18 E5
Munterconnacht Cavan 46 B8
Murntown/ Murrintown
Wexfd..................................15 N5
Murreagh/ An Mhuirioch
Kerry 8 D4
Murrisk/ Muraisc Mayo........41 K8
Murroe Limrck....................19 J4
Myshall/ Míseal Carlow 22 E3

N

Naas/ An Nás Kildre 38 G11
Na Dúnaibh/ Downings
Donegl.................................65 K6
Na Forbacha/ Furbo
Galway 33 Q10
Naran Donegl......................58 F4
Narraghmore/ An Fhorrach
Mhór Kildre.........................30 C5
National Aquatic Centre &
AquaZone Dublin 39 L7
National Botanic Gardens
C Dubl..................................39 M7
National Gallery of Ireland
C Dubl..................................39 N8
National Library of Ireland
C Dubl..................................39 N8
National Museum of Ireland
(Archaeology) C Dubl.........39 N8
National Museum of Ireland
(Decorative Arts)
C Dubl..................................39 M8
National Museum of Ireland
(Natural History)
C Dubl..................................39 N8
National Print Museum
C Dubl..................................39 N8
National Sea Life Centre
Wicklw 39 Q11
National Wax Museum Plus
C Dubl..................................39 N8
Naul Dublin.........................39 M2
Navan/ An Uaimh Meath 46 G11
Neale Mayo.........................33 Q3
Nenagh/ An tAonach
Tippry 27 L10
Newbawn Wexfd................15 J4
New Birmingham/ Gleann
an Ghuail Tippry 20 F5
Newbliss/ Cúil Darach
Monhan 54 H9
Newbridge Limrck..............17 P6
Newbridge/ Droichead Nua
Galway 35 M4
Newbridge/ Droichead Nua
Kildre 30 D2
Newbuildings D & S............66 C11
Newcastle Dublin 39 J9
Newcastle Galway..............34 H8
Newcastle NM & D..............57 K7
Newcastle Tippry 13 K6
Newcastle/ An Caisleán Nua
Wicklw 31 N5
Newcastle West/ An Caisleán
Nua Limrck..........................17 N9
New Garden Limrck............18 H3
Newgrange Meath 47 K10
New Inn Galway..................35 L9
New Inn/ Loch Ceann
Tippry 20 C9
Newmarket Kilken.............21 M8
Newmarket/ Áth Trasna
Cork 10 H4
Newmarket on Fergus/
Cora Chaitlín Clare.............18 B2
Newmills Cork 4 H9
Newmills Donegl.................59 P2
Newmills M Ulst.................61 N10
Newport/ An Port Nua
Tippry 19 J3
Newport/ Baile Uí Fhiacháin
Mayo 41 L6
New Ross/ Ros Mhic Thriúin
Wexfd..................................22 C10
Newry NM & D 56 D8
Newtown Carlow 22 D5
Newtown Dublin 39 N10
Newtown Galway................34 F8
Newtown Galway................35 L5
Newtown Kildre 29 P3
Newtown Kildre 30 D4
Newtown Kildre 30 F3

Newtown Kildre 38 F7
Newtown Kildre 39 J8
Newtown Laois...................29 L10
Newtown Meath.................46 H7
Newtown Offaly..................27 Q2
Newtown Offaly..................36 D10
Newtown Offaly..................36 H7
Newtown Roscom...............44 C8
Newtown Sligo...................51 N5
Newtown Tippry.................27 K9
Newtown Watfd..................13 R7
Newtown Wexfd.................14 F5
Newtown Wexfd.................15 J7
Newtownabbey A & N.........63 J7
Newtownards A & ND.........63 M9
Newtownbutler F & O.........54 E8
Newtowncashel Longfd.....36 D3
Newtown Crommelin
E Antr..................................68 C10
Newtown Cunningham/
An Baile Nua Donegl.............65 Q10
Newtownforbes/ An Lios
Breac Longfd.......................44 F9
Newtownhamilton
NM & D................................55 Q8
Newtownmountkennedy/
Baile an Chinnéidigh
Wicklw 31 N4
Newtownstewart D & S......60 E6
New Twopothouse Cork.....11 M5
Nicker Limrck......................19 K6
Ninemilehouse Tippry........21 J9
Nobber/ An Obair Meath.....46 F7
Nohoval Cork........................6 B11
North Down Museum
A & ND..................................63 N7
Nurney Kildre 29 P4
Nursetown More Cork........11 M7

O

O'Briensbridge/ Droichead Uí
Bhriain Clare......................18 H2
O'Callaghansmills Clare 26 D10
Ogonnelloe Clare...............26 G9
Oileán Árann/ Aran Islands
Galway 24 B4
Oileán Chléire/ Cape Clear
Island Cork 3 Q12
Oilgate/ Maolán na nGabhar
Wexfd..................................22 H9
Old Bushmills Distillery
CC & G.................................67 N5
Oldcastle/ An Seanchaisleán
Meath..................................45 Q8
Old Jameson Distillery
C Dubl..................................39 M8
Old Kilcullen Kildre...........30 D4
Old Kilmeadan Watfd.........14 C6
Old Leighlin Carlow............21 Q2
Old Mill E Antr 63 K2
Old Pallas Limrck...............19 K7
Old Pound Laois.................29 L4
Old Ross/ Seanros Wexfd....22 D10
Oldtown Dublin 39 M4
Oldtown Roscom................36 D7
Omagh F & O......................60 F9
Omeath/ Ó Méith Louth......56 E10
Oola/ Úlla Limrck................19 L7
Oram Monhan 55 P9
Oranmore/ Órán Mór
Galway 34 E10
Oristown/ Baile Órthaí
Meath..................................46 E9
Oughterard/ Uachtar Ard
Galway 33 P6
Oulart/ An tAbhallort
Wexfd..................................15 Q7
Our Lady's Island Wexfd.....15 Q7
Ovens Cork...........................5 M2
Owenahincha Cork.............4 H9
Owning Kilken....................14 A3

P

Palatine Carlow..................30 C10
Pallas Cork............................3 K5
Pallasgreen/ Pailis Ghréine
Limrck.................................19 K6
Pallaskenry Limrck............18 C4
Palmerston Dublin.............39 L8
Park D & S...........................60 H3
Parke Mayo........................42 B5
Parkgate A & N...................62 G6

Parteen Clare....18 F3
Partry Mayo....41 Q10
Passage East/ An Pasáiste Watfd....14 G6
Passage West/ An Pasáiste Cork....6 C8
Patrickswell/ Tobar Phádraig Limrck....18 E6
Paulstown/ Baile Phóil Kilken....21 Q4
Paulstown Services Kilken....21 Q4
Pettigo/ Paiteagó Donegl....59 P10
Phelim's Cross Laois....29 L8
Philipstown Louth....47 K7
Phoenix Park C Dubl....39 M7
Piercetown Cork....5 Q5
Piercetown Wexfd....15 N5
Piltown/ Baile an Phoill Kilken....14 B4
Piperstown Louth....47 L8
Plumbridge D & S....60 F5
Poles Cavan....45 N4
Pollagh Mayo....40 D4
Pollagh Offaly....36 G9
Poll an tSomais/ Pollatomish Mayo....48 H6
Pollardstown Cork....12 D6
Pollatomish/ Poll an tSomais Mayo....48 H6
Pomeroy M Ulst....61 K9
Pontoon Mayo....42 B4
Portadown AB & C....56 C3
Portaferry A & ND....57 P3
Portahack Donegl....66 E3
Portarlington/ Cúil an tSúdaire Laois....29 K3
Portavogie A & ND....57 R2
Portballintrae CC & G....67 N5
Portbradden CC & G....67 Q5
Portglenone E Antr....62 B3
Port Laoise/ Portlaoise Laois....29 J6
Portlaw/ Port Lách Watfd....14 B5
Portmagee/ An Caladh Kerry....8 D11
Portmarnock/ Port Mearnóg Dublin....39 P6
Portnablagh/ Port na Bláiche Donegl....65 J6
Portnakilly Mayo....40 E8
Portnoo Donegl....58 E4
Portrane Dublin....39 Q4
Portroe/ An Port Rua Tippry....27 J9
Portrush CC & G....67 M5
Portsalon/ Port an tSalainn Donegl....65 N5
Portstewart CC & G....67 L6
Portumna/ Port Omna Galway....27 L5
Poulnamucky Tippry....20 D10
Powerscourt House & Gardens Wicklw....31 M2
Poyntzpass AB & C....56 D6
Prehen D & S....66 C10
Prosperous/ An Chorrchoill Kildre....38 F9
Puckaun/ Pocán Tippry....27 K8
Pullincha Cork....3 J7

Q

Quakers Cross Roads Cork....4 G9
Quay Village Mayo....50 F9
Quigley's Point Donegl....66 E7
Quilty Clare....24 F11
Quin/ Cuinche Clare....25 P11
Quitrent Cork....11 Q3

R

Raghly Sligo....51 M5
Raghrabeg Roscom....36 B9
Rahan Offaly....37 J9
Rahara Roscom....36 B4
Raharney/ Ráth Fhearna Wmeath....38 A4
Raheen Laois....38 H7
Raheen/ An Ráithín Wexfd....15 J3
Raheen Cross Roads Cork....4 E10
Raheny C Dubl....39 P7

Raholp NM & D....57 N4
Ráith/ Ray Donegl....64 H7
Raloo E Antr....63 K4
Ramelton/ Ráth Mealtain Donegl....65 N9
Ramoy Monhan....54 H7
Ramsgrange Wexfd....14 G6
Randalstown A & N....62 D5
Raphoe/ Ráth Bhoth Donegl....60 B3
Rasharkin CC & G....67 P11
Rathangan/ Ráth Iomgháin Kildre....38 C11
Rathbeggan Meath....39 J5
Rathcairn/ Ráth Chairn Meath....38 E2
Ráth Chairn/ Rathcairn Meath....38 E2
Rathcoffey Kildre....38 G8
Rathcoole/ Ráth Cúil Dublin....39 K9
Rathcormac/ Ráth Chormaic Cork....6 D3
Rathdangan Wicklw....30 G8
Rathdowney/ Ráth Domhnaigh Laois....28 E10
Rathdrum/ Ráth Droma Wicklw....31 L8
Rathfarnham Dublin....39 M9
Ráth Fhearna/ Raharney Wmeath....38 A4
Rathfriland AB & C....56 F7
Rathgarogue Wexfd....22 D9
Rathgormuck Watfd....13 P5
Rathkeale/ Ráth Caola Limrck....17 Q7
Rathlin Island CC & G....68 C3
Rathmawe Meath....38 H3
Rathmolyon Meath....38 E5
Rathmore/ An Ráth Mhór Kerry....10 E7
Rathmore/ An Ráth Mhór Kildre....39 J11
Rathmullan/ Ráth Maoláin Donegl....65 P8
Rathnew/ Ráth Naoi Wicklw....31 N6
Rathnure Wexfd....22 E8
Rathowen/ Ráth Eoghain Wmeath....45 K11
Rathvilly/ Ráth Bhile Carlow....30 E9
Rathwire Wmeath....37 Q4
Ratoath/ Ráth Tó Meath....39 K4
Ravernet L & C....62 H11
Ray/ Ráith Donegl....64 H7
Recess/ Sraith Salach Galway....33 J5
Redcastle Donegl....66 F6
Redcross/ An Chrois Dhearg Wicklw....31 M9
Redhills/ An Cnoc Rua Cavan....54 E10
Redmonds Bridge Wicklw....30 F8
Reen Kerry....3 L7
Reenascreena Cork....4 G8
Reenroe Cork....2 G7
Rerrin Cork....3 K8
Rhode/ Ród Offaly....37 P8
Richhill AB & C....55 Q4
Ring/ An Rinn Watfd....7 N4
Ringaskiddy/ Rinn an Scidigh Cork....6 C9
Ringville Kilken....14 F5
Riverchapel Wexfd....23 M4
Riverstick/ Áth an Mhaide Cork....5 Q5
Riverstown Cork....6 B6
Riverstown Offaly....27 Q5
Riverstown/ Baile idir dhá Abhainn Sligo....52 L9
Robeen Mayo....42 B10
Roberts Cove/ Cuainín Riobaird Cork....6 C11
Robertstown/ Baile Riobaird Kildre....38 E9
Robinstown Meath....38 F2
Rochfortbridge Wmeath....37 N6
Rockcorry/ Buíochar Monhan....55 J10
Rock of Cashel Tippry....20 C7
Rolestown/ Baile an Rólaigh Dublin....39 M4
Roonah Quay Mayo....40 F8
Roosky/ Rúscaigh Roscom....44 D7
Rosahane Bridge Wicklw....31 J9

Ros an Mhíl/ Rossaveel Galway....33 L9
Rosbercon Wexfd....22 C10
Roscam C Gal....34 E9
Roscommon/ Ros Comáin Roscom....35 Q2
Roscrea/ Ros Cré Tippry....28 B8
Rosegreen Tippry....20 D8
Rosenallis Laois....28 G4
Roskelton Cross Laois....28 G7
Ross Mayo....41 Q5
Rossadrehid Tippry....19 N10
Rossaveel/ Ros an Mhíl Galway....33 L9
Rossbaun Laois....28 D7
Ross Behy Kerry....9 J7
Rosscahill Galway....33 Q7
Rosscarbery/ Ros Ó gCairbre Cork....4 G9
Ross Castle Kerry....9 Q8
Rossdorragha Laois....28 D7
Rossduff Watfd....14 F7
Rosses Point/ An Ros Sligo....51 N6
Rossinver Leitrm....53 J4
Rosslare/ Ros Láir Wexfd....15 Q4
Rosslare Harbour Wexfd....15 Q6
Rosslea F & O....54 G7
Rossnowlagh Donegl....59 J10
Rostrevor NM & D....56 F10
Roundstone/ Cloch na Rón Galway....32 F6
Roundwood/ An Tóchar Wicklw....31 L5
Rousky F & O....60 G6
Ruan Clare....25 M8
Rush/ An Ros Dublin....39 Q4
Rushin Cross Laois....28 F6
Russborough House & Parklands Wicklw....30 G3
Ryefield Cavan....46 B8
Rylane Kerry....17 J10
Rylane Cross Cork....11 K9

S

Saggart Dublin....39 K9
Saintfield NM & D....57 L2
St Johnston/ Baile Suingean Donegl....60 C2
St Margaret's Dublin....39 M6
St Mullins Carlow....22 C8
St Patrick Centre NM & D....57 M5
St Patrick's Cathedral C Dubl....39 N8
Saleen Cork....6 E8
Sallins/ Na Solláin Kildre....38 G10
Sallybrook Cork....6 B6
Salthill C Gal....34 C10
Saltmills Wexfd....14 H7
Sandholes M Ulst....61 M9
Sandpit Louth....47 M8
Sandycove Cork....5 P7
Santry C Dubl....39 N7
Saul NM & D....57 N4
Scarriff/ An Scairbh Clare....26 F9
Scartaglin/ Scairteach an Ghlinne Kerry....10 B5
Scarva NM & D....56 D5
School Cross Laois....28 D10
Schull/ An Scoil Cork....3 P10
Science Gallery C Dubl....39 N8
Scotch Street AB & C....56 B2
Scotshouse Monhan....54 F10
Scotstown/ Baile an Scotaigh Monhan....55 J6
Scrahanagaur Kerry....3 J3
Scramoge Roscom....44 C9
Screen Wexfd....23 K9
Seaforde NM & D....57 L5
Seapoint Louth....47 N8
Semple Stadium Tippry....20 D4
Seskinore F & O....60 F11
Shanagarry Cork....6 G8
Shanaglish Galway....25 P6
Shanagolden/ Seanghualainn Limrck....17 N6
Shanbally/ An Seanbhaile Cork....6 C9
Shanballymore/ An Seanbhaile Mór Cork....11 Q4
Shankill/ Seanchill Dublin....39 Q10
Shannon/ Sionainn Clare....18 C3
Shannon Airport Clare....18 B3

Shannonbridge/ Droichead na Sionainne Offaly....36 C9
Shannon Harbour Offaly....36 D11
Shannonvale Cork....5 J8
Sheffield Cross Laois....29 J6
Shercock/ Searcóg Cavan....46 D3
Sherkin Island Cork....4 B12
Shillelagh/ Síol Éalaigh Wicklw....22 H2
Shinrone/ Suí an Róin Offaly....27 Q7
Shrigley NM & D....57 N3
Shrule/ Shruthair Mayo....34 C4
Silverbridge NM & D....56 B10
Silvermines/ Béal Átha Gabhann Tippry....27 K11
Simonstown Wmeath....45 M10
Sion Mills D & S....60 C5
Sixmilebridge/ Droichead Abhann Ó gCearnaigh Clare....18 D2
Sixmilecross F & O....60 H10
Skeeheenarinky Tippry....12 F5
Skehanagh Galway....35 J6
Skeheen Mayo....43 J5
Skerries/ Na Sceirí Dublin....39 Q2
Skerries Mills Dublin....39 Q3
Skibbereen/ An Sciobairín Cork....4 D10
Skreen Meath....39 J2
Slade/ An Slaod Wexfd....14 G9
Slane/ Baile Shláine Meath....47 J10
Slane Castle Meath....46 H10
Slatta Roscom....44 D8
Slieve Gullion Forest Park NM & D....56 C9
Slieve League Cliffs Donegl....58 B8
Slieverue Kilken....14 C6
Sligo/ Sligeach Sligo....52 D6
Sligo Airport Sligo....51 N6
Smithborough Monhan....54 H7
Sneem/ An Snaidhm Kerry....3 J3
Snugborough Bridge Wicklw....30 G6
Somer Galway....35 P10
Sooey Sligo....52 E9
Spa Kerry....9 M2
Spa NM & D....57 K4
Spanish Point/ Rinn na Spáinneach Clare....24 F10
Spaville Watfd....13 M4
Spiddal/ An Spidéal Galway....33 P10
Springfield F & O....53 P4
Srah Offaly....36 G9
Srah/ An tSraith Mayo....48 F8
Srahnamanragh Mayo....48 H11
Sraith Salach/ Recess Galway....33 J5
Stabannan Louth....47 K6
Stamullen Dublin....47 M11
Staplestown Kildre....38 F8
Stepaside/ An Céime Dublin....39 N10
Stewartstown M Ulst....61 P9
Stillorgan Dublin....39 P9
Stonehall Limrck....18 C5
Stonepark Donegl....59 J8
Stonepark Longfd....44 F10
Stoneyford Kilken....21 M7
Stoneyford L & C....62 G9
Strabane D & S....60 C4
Stradbally Kerry....8 H3
Stradbally/ An Sráidbhaile Laois....29 L6
Stradbally/ An tSráidbhaile Watfd....13 Q3
Stradone/ Sraith an Domhain Cavan....45 P4
Straffan Kildre....38 H8
Straid A & N....63 J5
Straidarran D & S....60 H2
Strandhill/ An Leathros Sligo....51 N6
Strangford NM & D....57 P4
Stranocum CC & G....67 Q7
Stranorlar/ Srath an Urláir Donegl....59 P4
Stratford/ Áth na Sráide Wicklw....30 E7
Streedagh Sligo....51 N3
Street/ Straid Wmeath....45 K10
Strokestown/ Béal na mBuillí Roscom....44 B8